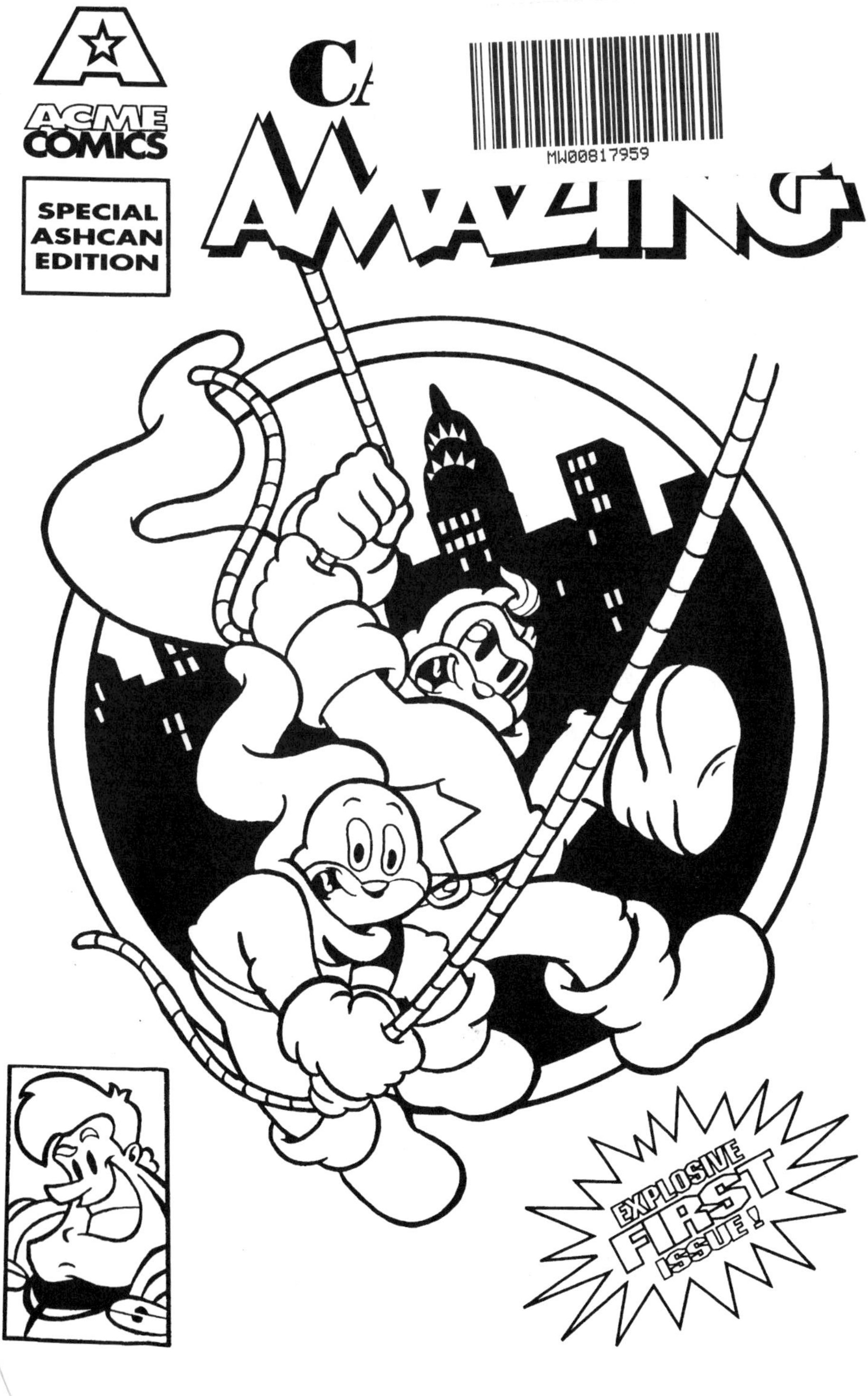
ACME COMICS
SPECIAL ASHCAN EDITION
CA
M
AMAZING
EXPLOSIVE FIRST ISSUE!

For Chris
Thanks for kicking my butt!

CAPTAIN AMAZING™

EPISODE ONE:
CLASH OF THE TITAN

FOR IMAGE COMICS:
ERIK LARSEN:
PUBLISHER
TODD MCFARLANE:
PRESIDENT
MARC SILVESTRI:
CEO
JIM VALENTINO:
VICE PRESIDENT
ERIC STEPHENSON:
EXEC DIRECTOR
JIM DEMONAKOS:
PR & MARKETING
MIA MACHATTON:
ACCOUNT MANAGER
TRACI HUI:
ADMIN ASSISTANT
JOE KEATINGE:
TRAFFIC MANAGER
ALLEN HUI:
PRODUCTION MANAGER
JONATHAN CHAN:
PRODUCTION ARTIST
DREW GILL:
PRODUCTION ARTIST

www.imagecomics.com

BY:
SCOTT KURTZ &
CHRIS JACKSON

· F O R E W O R D ·

This book has a great story behind it.

The year is 1994 and I'm a college drop-out. I had attended the University of North Texas for about three years right out of high-school, lost interest and quit. I was studying advertising art, but I was more interested in Cartooning. I spent more time partying with my friends and working on my comic strip for the student paper than I did my studies.

I was working at a sign company, moving big sheets of Plexiglas around a hot warehouse and dreaming of a job in the air-conditioned graphics department. My parents were disappointed, I had no money, no plans, and no realistic ambitions. Things were far from perfect.

I did, however, meet my wife. She worked at the sign company too. We became friends, started dating and everything turned around for me. Sure I still had a crappy job and no money, but I was in love so who cared? I proposed on Christmas Eve, 2004 and we set a date for February, 2006.

So, with a wedding looming in the distance, and knowing that I really had no way of supporting this woman, I did the smart thing: I moved into an apartment with my college buddy and decided to work on a comic book with him.

Chris Jackson was also attending UNT. He also had a comic strip in the student paper; the hilarious and sublime "Near Whomp." Chris always felt that I had the potential to make it with my cartooning. But with marriage and responsibility on the horizon, he felt I only had one year left to make something happen. Soon life would intervene and I would have to give up on such irresponsible ambitions.

He proposed we rent an apartment together, set up a detailed production schedule and create a 50 page comic book based on my student comic strip, Captain Amazing.

He would help me co-write the story and act as editor and drill sergeant. He would make sure I stuck to the schedule and didn't do what I normally do; lose interest and quit.

If I couldn't find the motivation internally to make this happen, he would provide it *externally!*

For seven months we worked on the book. Rewrites, thumbnails, redrawing pages over and over until I got it just the way Chris liked it. There were arguments about broken promises and missed deadlines. I wanted to give up halfway through the process but Chris wouldn't let that happen. I made Chris' life a living hell for that year, but by the end of July, we had a finished book.

And it wasn't too bad, either. If we did say so ourselves.

We printed 600 copies of our mini-comic (of course, back then, they didn't call them mini-comics. They were called "ashcan editions"), made some tee-shirts to sell along side them and started hitting local Dallas comic conventions. We got a luke warm response.

Around that time, a contact I had made over at Wildstorm Comics encouraged me to attend the 1995 San Diego Comicon. I was reluctant to attend, but Chris and my friend Colby were pushing me to. Colby even offered to pay my way to the show. I had a completed comic, a contact in a prestigious comic book company and the largest comic book convention waiting for me in San Diego. They weren't going to let me pass up this opportunity.

Of all the publishers and professionals I showed this book to (including my contacts) only Larry Marder showed any interest in it at all. I knew Larry Marder as the creator of the independent comic book BEAN WORLD. What I didn't know was that Larry had a day job.

He was Executive Director of Image Comics.

"Nice line work, I like this." Larry said as he thumbed through this book. "Here's my card. Call me after the show when I'm back in the office. I want to talk to you about this book. Just call me in a week or two."

I returned home convinced that we had done it. I would wait until next week and call Larry. I was going to be a published cartoonist.

Of course, that never happened. Larry never took or returned my calls. I phoned the Image Central offices so many times that Larry's assistant actually demanded I not call anymore.

Now jump forward about ten years.

Somehow through the grace of God, and continued support from family and friends, I've managed to become a full-time cartoonist. And after a lot of hard work, I even got Image to publish my comic strips. But not Captain Amazing. The Captain went into storage with all my older ideas and drawings. It was my comic strip **Player Vs. Player** that would get the Image logo in the top left corner.

That is, until now.

This work is difficult for me to show you. It's not my most current or best work. It's eleven years old and a little difficult for me to look back at. I could have published this a year ago, but I was too nervous that people wouldn't like it.

But the Captain will always hold a special place in my heart. He was the comic strip I cut my teeth on, and I feel I owe it to him.

And so, eleven years later, Captain Amazing will finally complete his greatest feat: attending the San Diego Comicon as an Image Comic book.

Better late than never.

Scott R. Kurtz
June 2006

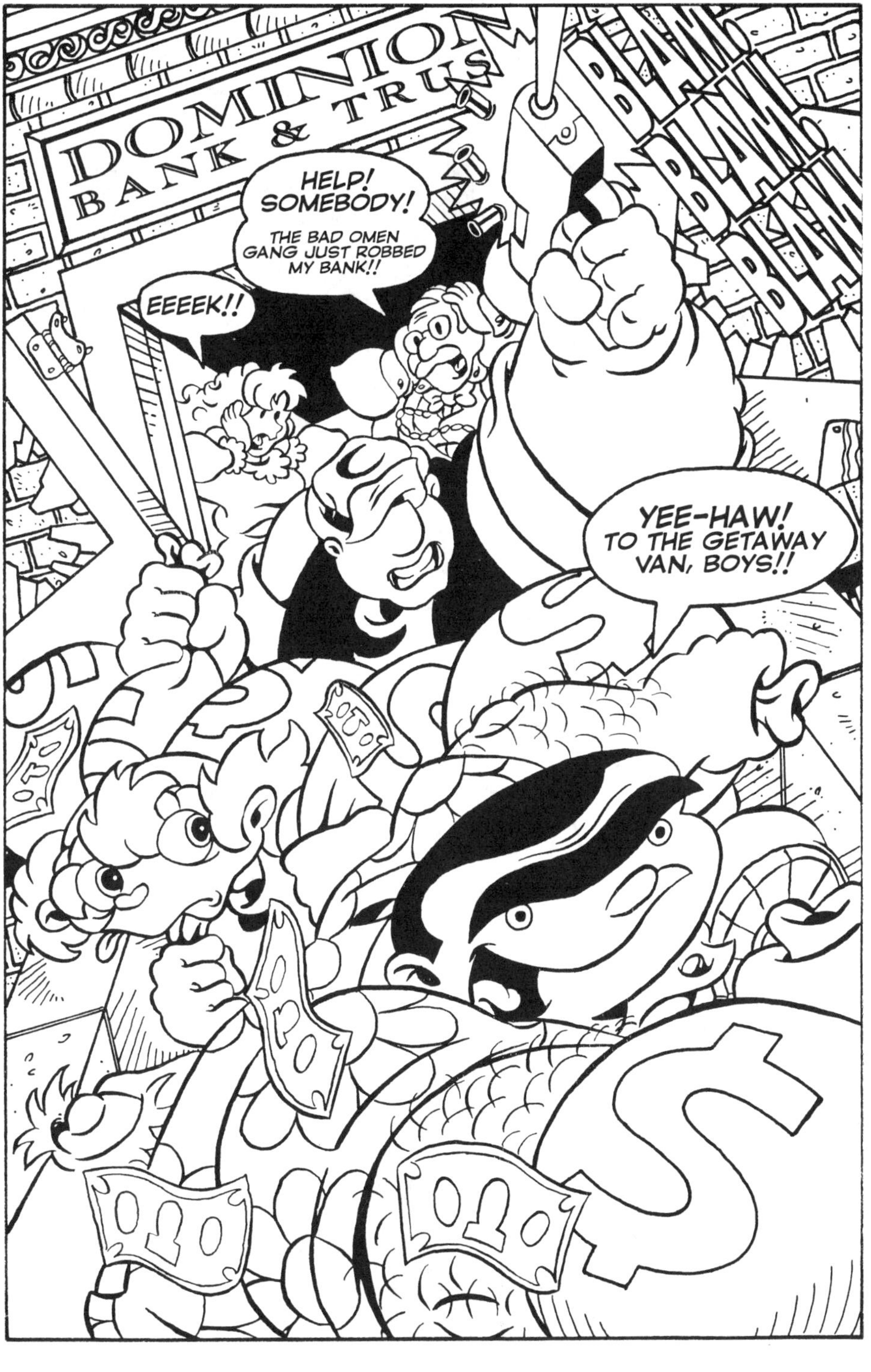
DOMINION BANK & TRUS
BLAM! BLAM! BLAM!
HELP! SOMEBODY! THE BAD OMEN GANG JUST ROBBED MY BANK!!
EEEEK!!
YEE-HAW! TO THE GETAWAY VAN, BOYS!!

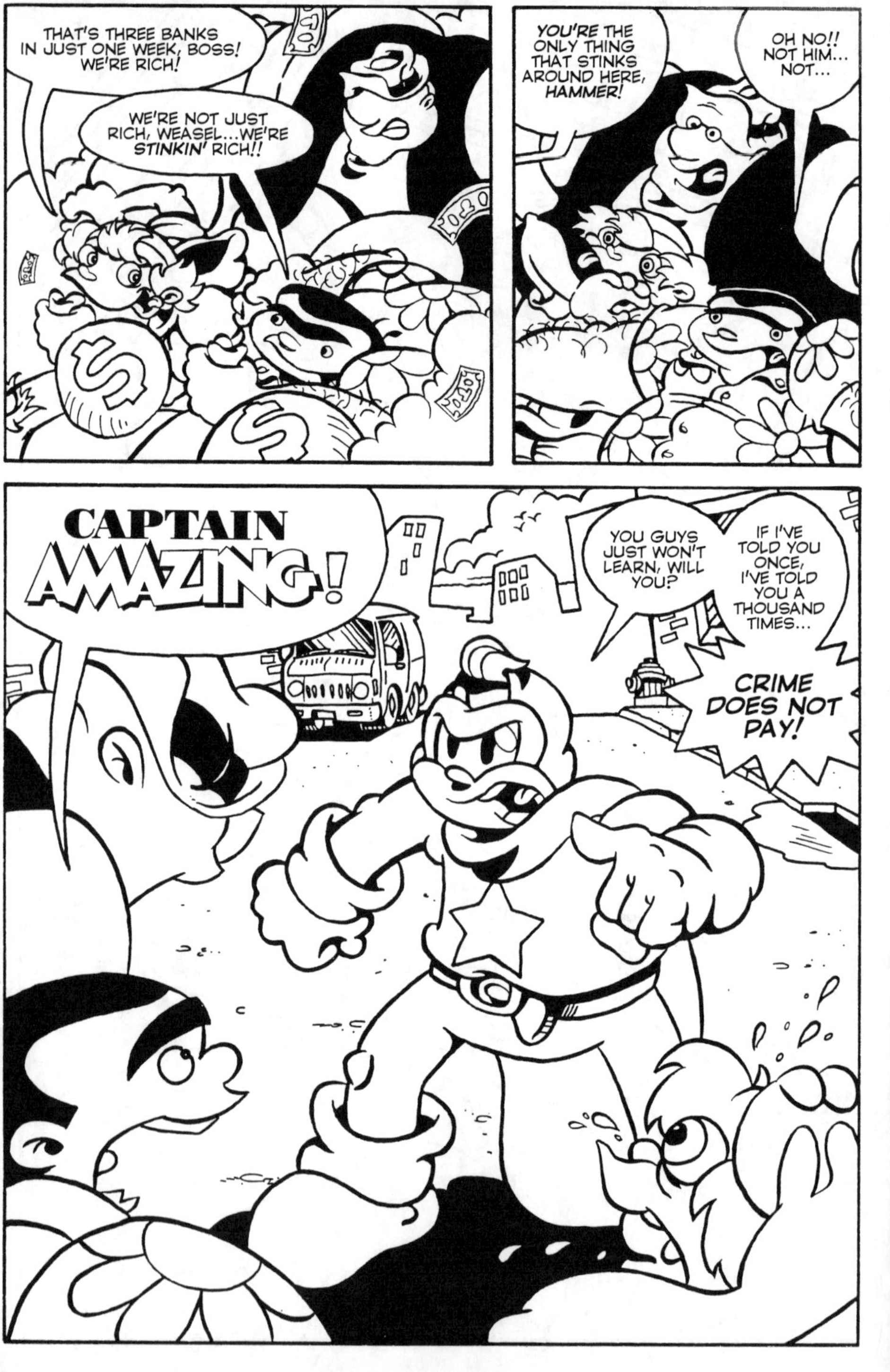
THAT'S THREE BANKS IN JUST ONE WEEK, BOSS! WE'RE RICH!
WE'RE NOT JUST RICH, WEASEL...WE'RE STINKIN' RICH!!
YOU'RE THE ONLY THING THAT STINKS AROUND HERE, HAMMER!
OH NO!! NOT HIM... NOT...
CAPTAIN AMAZING!
YOU GUYS JUST WON'T LEARN, WILL YOU?
IF I'VE TOLD YOU ONCE, I'VE TOLD YOU A THOUSAND TIMES...
CRIME DOES NOT PAY!

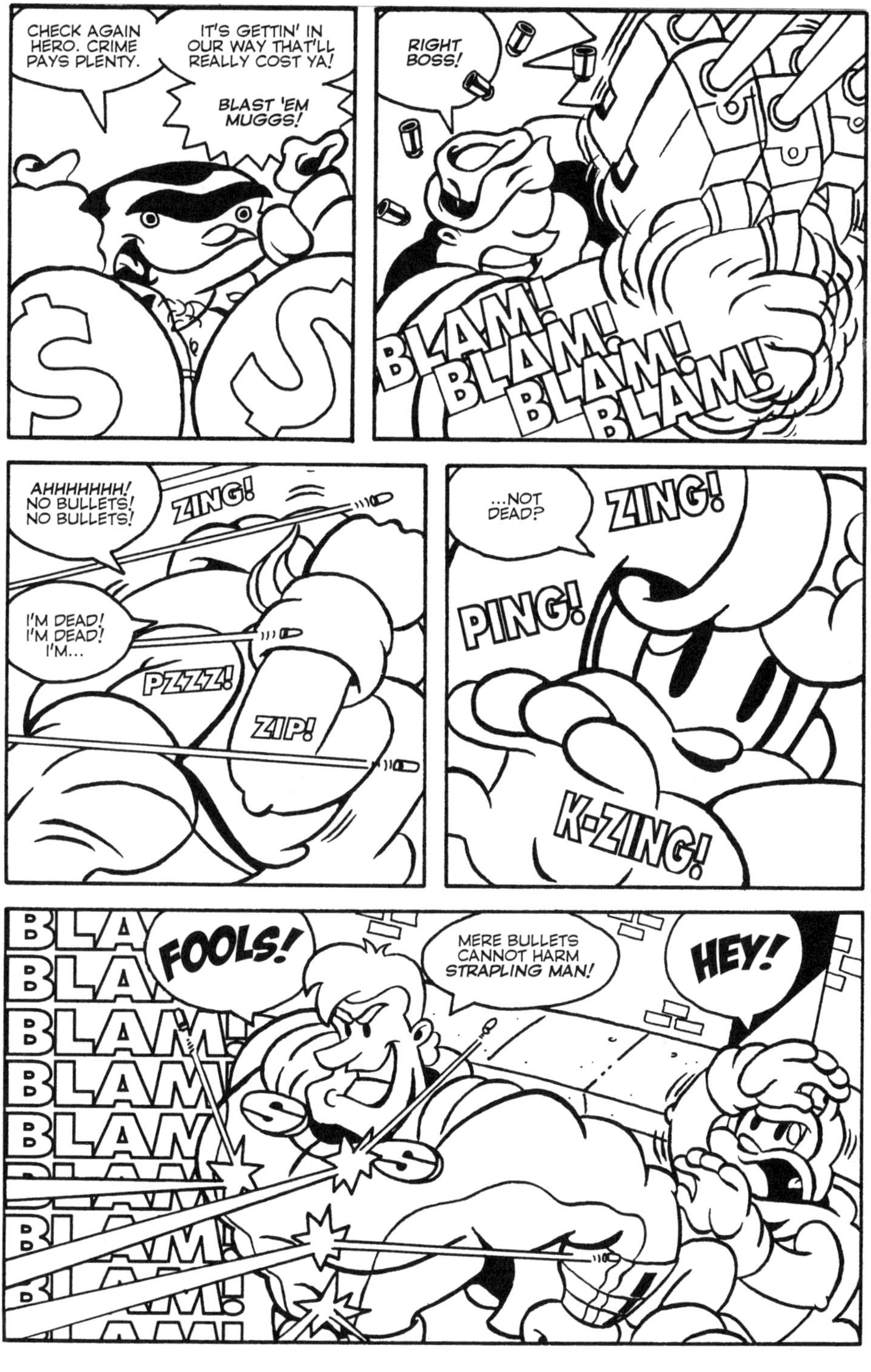
CHECK AGAIN HERO. CRIME PAYS PLENTY.
IT'S GETTIN' IN OUR WAY THAT'LL REALLY COST YA!
BLAST 'EM MUGGS!
RIGHT BOSS!
BLAM! BLAM! BLAM! BLAM!
AHHHHHHH! NO BULLETS! NO BULLETS!
ZING!
I'M DEAD! I'M DEAD! I'M...
PZZZZ!
ZIP!
...NOT DEAD?
ZING!
PING!
K-ZING!
FOOLS!
MERE BULLETS CANNOT HARM STRAPLING MAN!
HEY!
BLAM! BLAM! BLAM! BLAM! BLAM! BLAM! BLAM! BLAM!

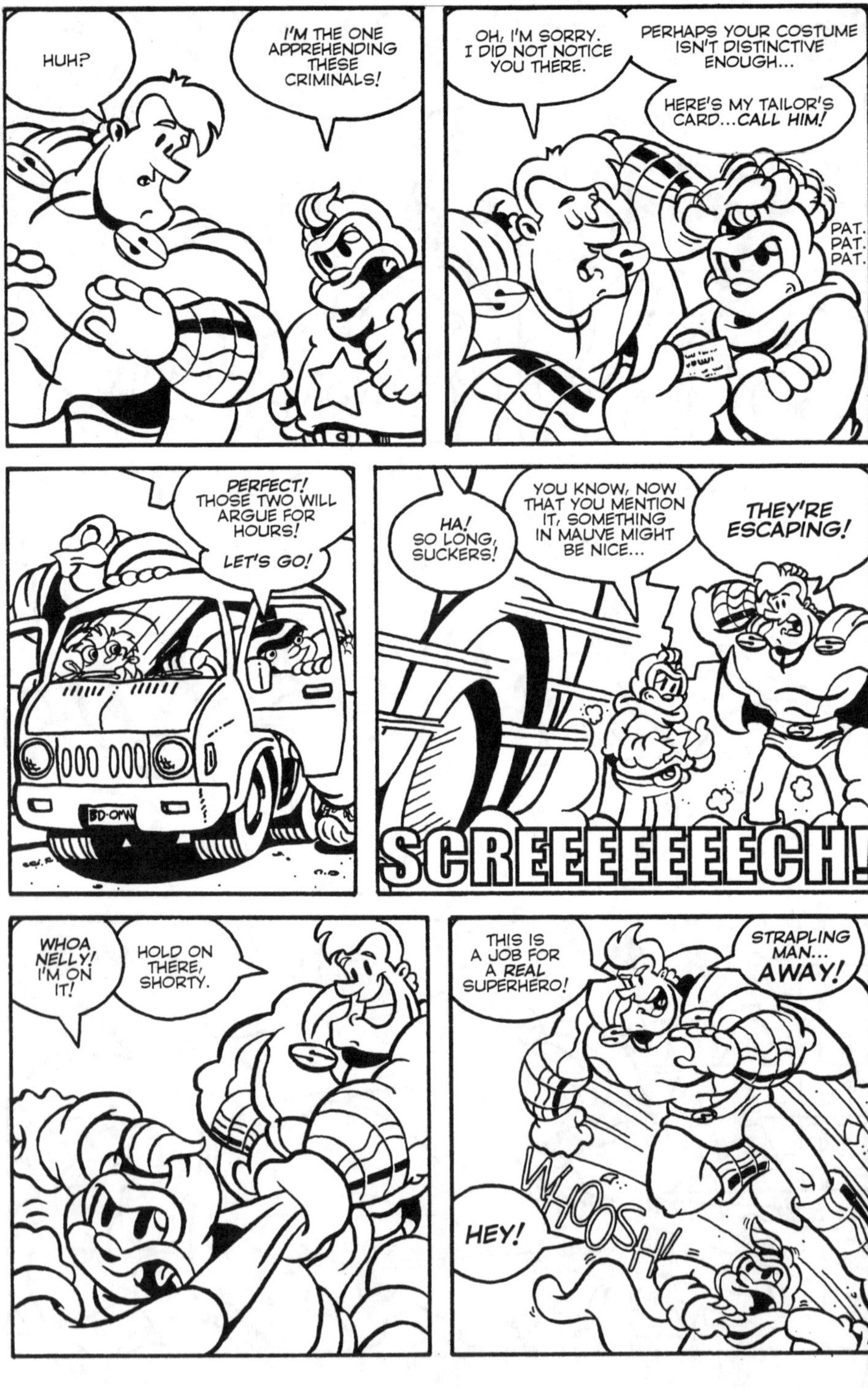
HUH?
I'M THE ONE APPREHENDING THESE CRIMINALS!
OH, I'M SORRY. I DID NOT NOTICE YOU THERE.
PERHAPS YOUR COSTUME ISN'T DISTINCTIVE ENOUGH...
HERE'S MY TAILOR'S CARD...CALL HIM!
PAT. PAT. PAT.
PERFECT! THOSE TWO WILL ARGUE FOR HOURS!
LET'S GO!
BD-OMW
HA! SO LONG, SUCKERS!
YOU KNOW, NOW THAT YOU MENTION IT, SOMETHING IN MAUVE MIGHT BE NICE...
THEY'RE ESCAPING!
SCREEEEEEEECH!
WHOA NELLY! I'M ON IT!
HOLD ON THERE, SHORTY.
THIS IS A JOB FOR A REAL SUPERHERO!
STRAPLING MAN... AWAY!
HEY!
WHOOSH!

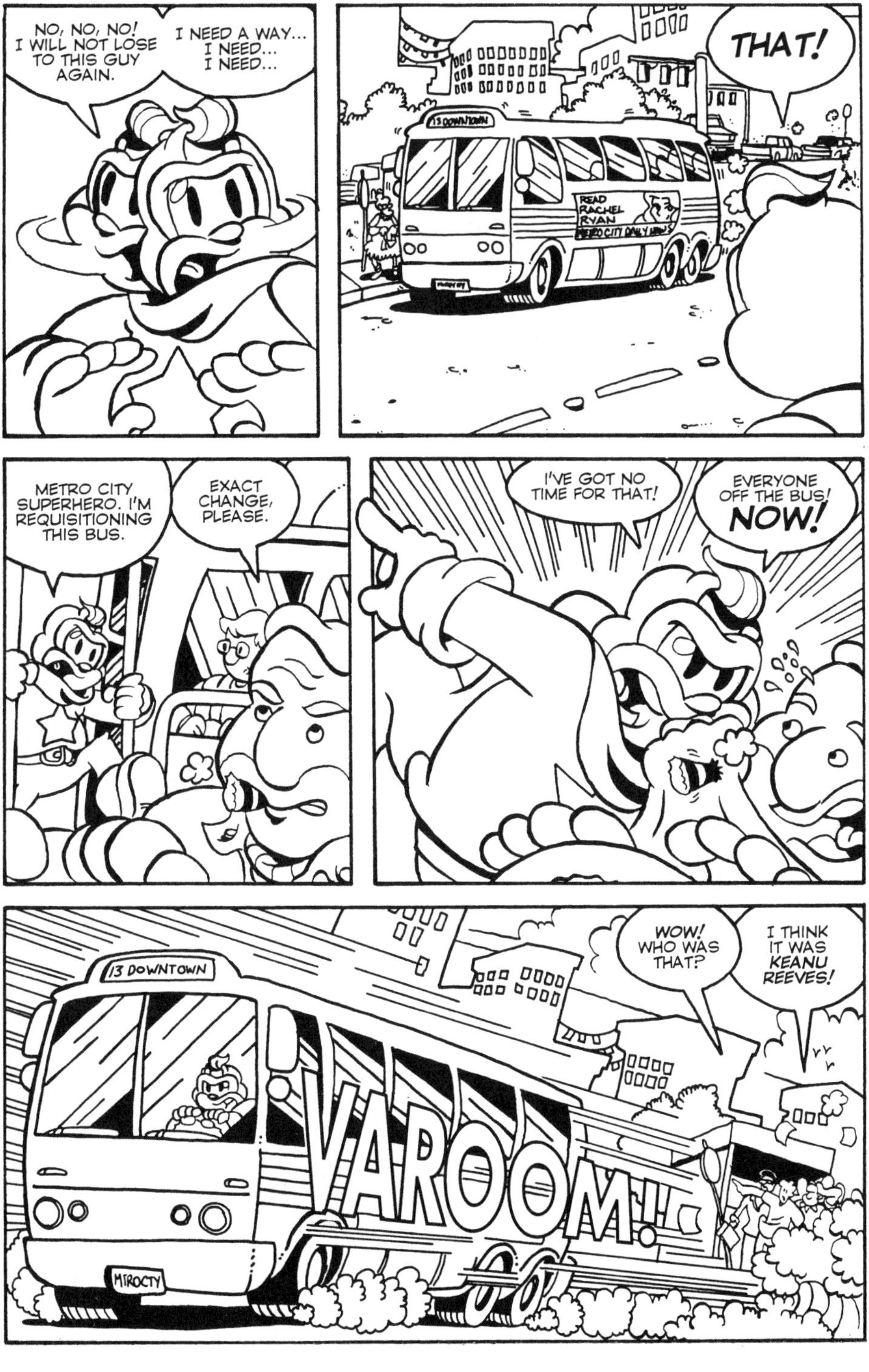
NO, NO, NO! I WILL NOT LOSE TO THIS GUY AGAIN.
I NEED A WAY... I NEED... I NEED...
THAT!
13 DOWNTOWN
READ RACHEL RYAN METRO CITY DAILY NEWS
METRO CITY SUPERHERO. I'M REQUISITIONING THIS BUS.
EXACT CHANGE, PLEASE.
I'VE GOT NO TIME FOR THAT!
EVERYONE OFF THE BUS! NOW!
13 DOWNTOWN
VAROOM!!
WOW! WHO WAS THAT?
I THINK IT WAS KEANU REEVES!
MTROCTY

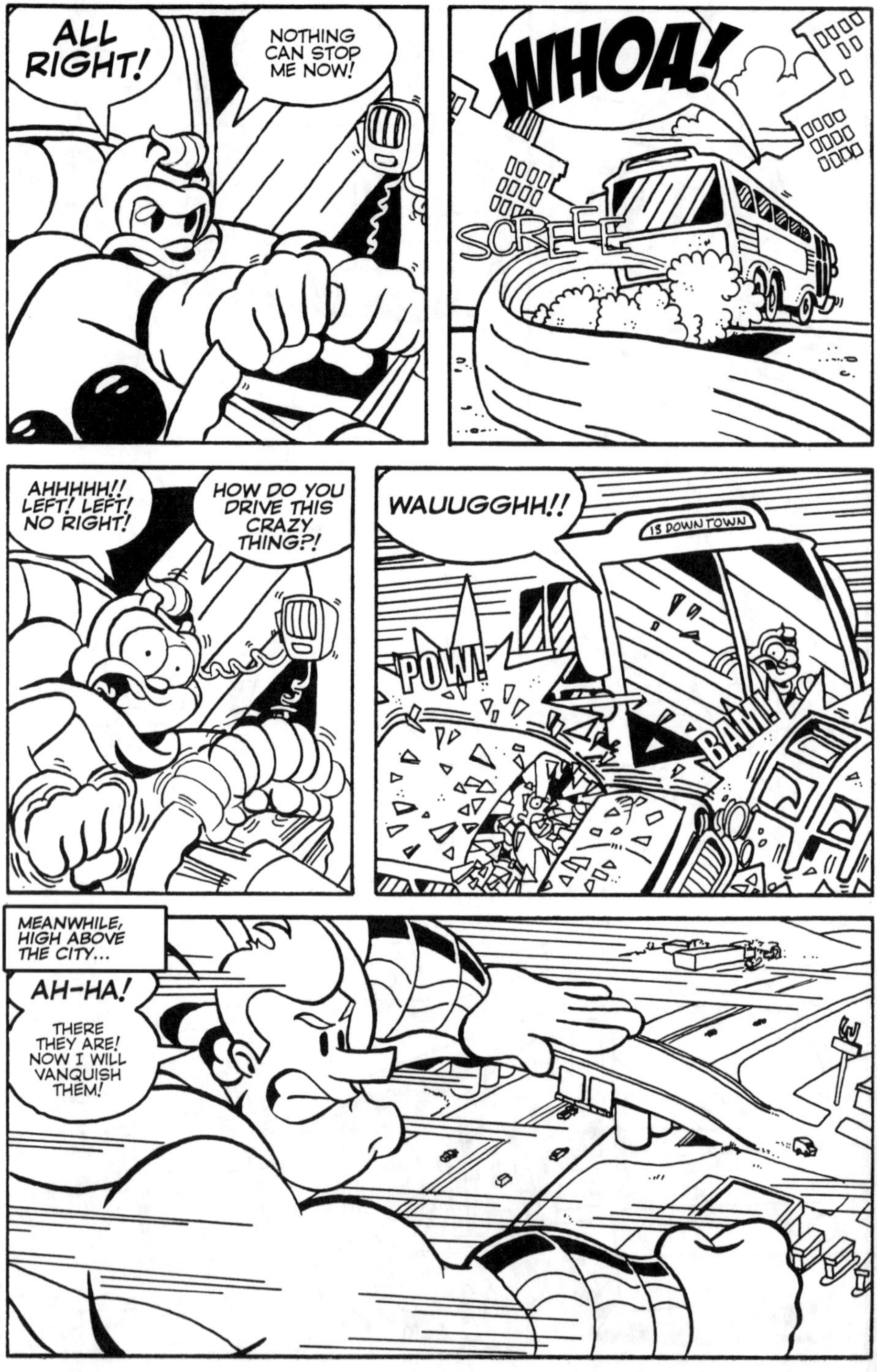
ALL RIGHT!
NOTHING CAN STOP ME NOW!
WHOA!
SCREEE
AHHHHH!! LEFT! LEFT! NO RIGHT!
HOW DO YOU DRIVE THIS CRAZY THING?!
WAUUGGHH!!
13 DOWNTOWN
POW!
BAM!
MEANWHILE, HIGH ABOVE THE CITY...
AH-HA!
THERE THEY ARE! NOW I WILL VANQUISH THEM!

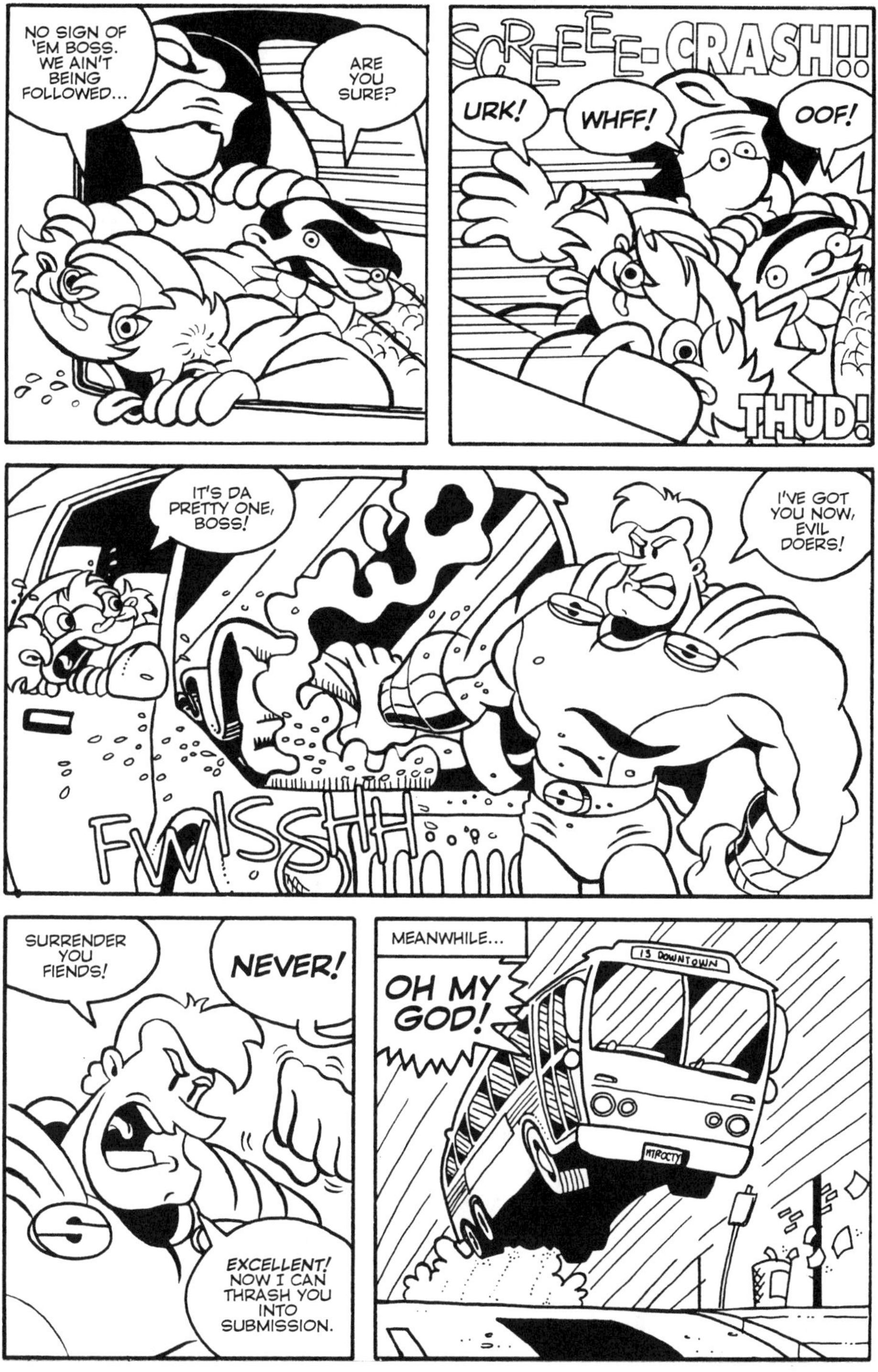
NO SIGN OF 'EM BOSS. WE AIN'T BEING FOLLOWED...
ARE YOU SURE?
SCREEEE-CRASH!!
URK!
WHFF!
OOF!
THUD!
IT'S DA PRETTY ONE, BOSS!
I'VE GOT YOU NOW, EVIL DOERS!
FWISSHH
SURRENDER YOU FIENDS!
NEVER!
EXCELLENT! NOW I CAN THRASH YOU INTO SUBMISSION.
MEANWHILE...
OH MY GOD!
13 DOWNTOWN

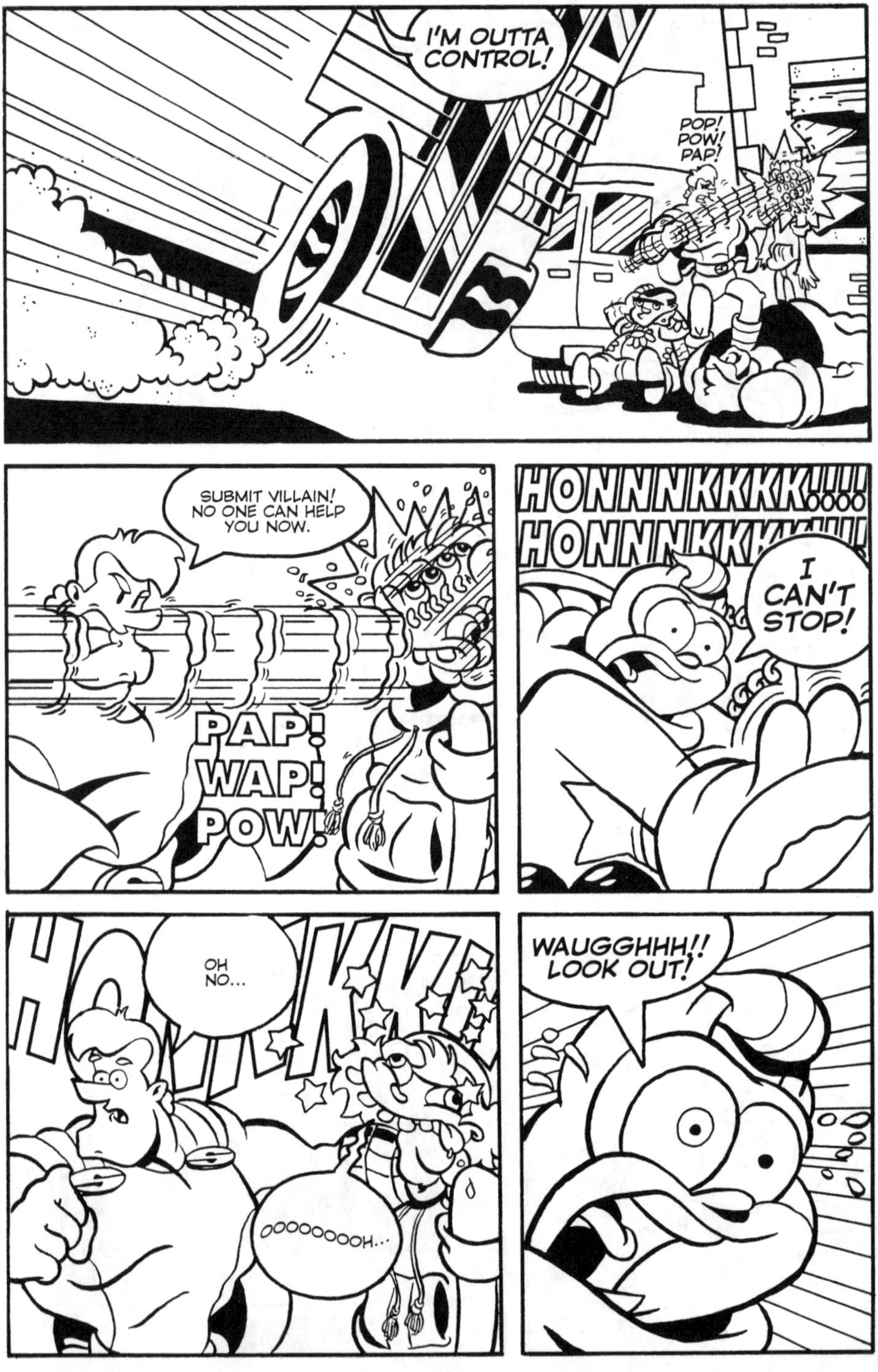
I'M OUTTA CONTROL!
POP! POW! PAP!
SUBMIT VILLAIN! NO ONE CAN HELP YOU NOW.
PAP! WAP! POW!
HONNNKKKK!!!!OOOO
HONNNKKKK!!!!
I CAN'T STOP!
OH NO...
OOOOOOOOH...
WAUGGHHH!! LOOK OUT!

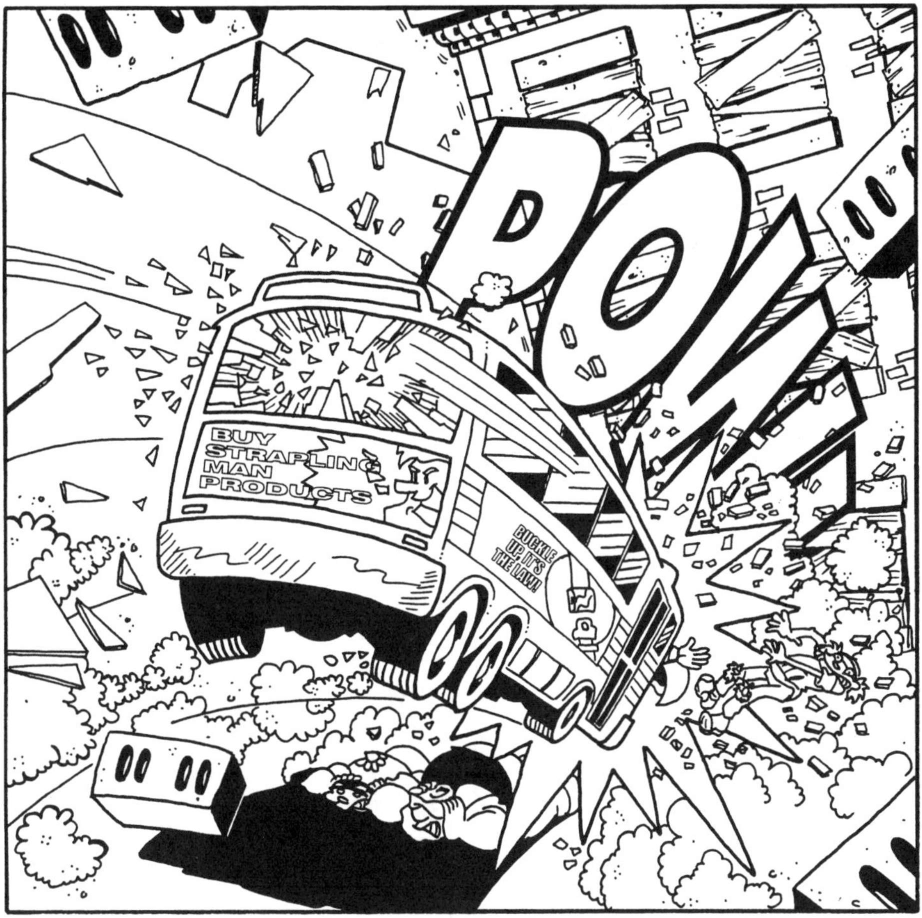
BUY STRAPLING MAN PRODUCTS
BUCKLE UP, IT'S THE LAW!

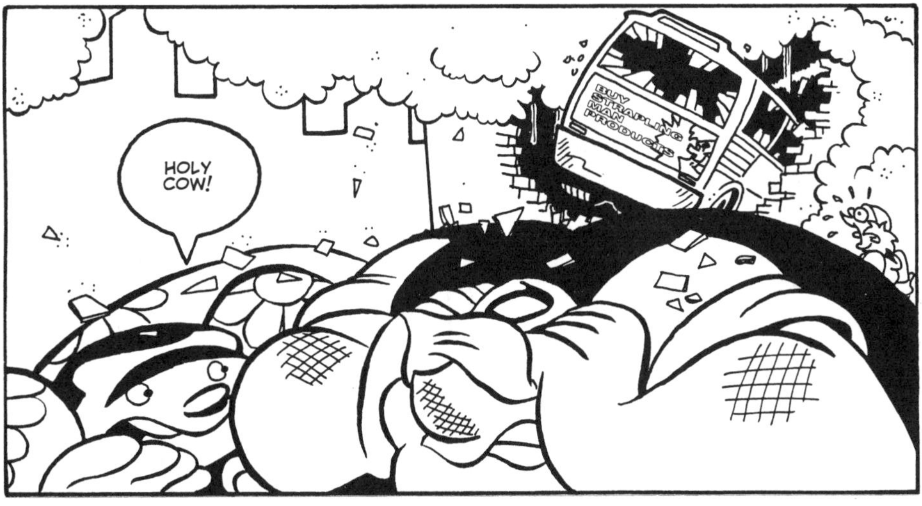
BUY STRAPLING MAN PRODUCTS
HOLY COW!

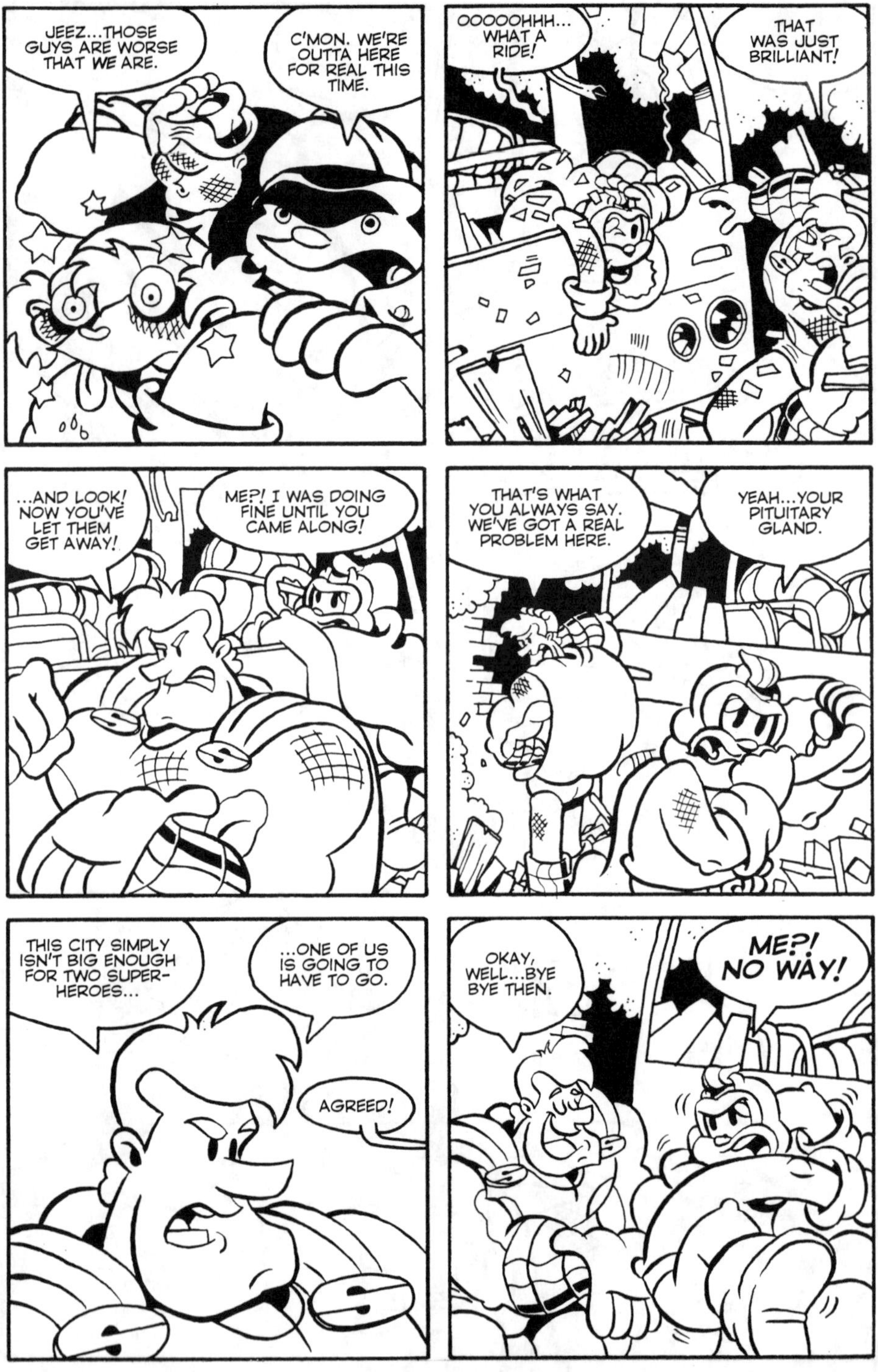
JEEZ...THOSE GUYS ARE WORSE THAT WE ARE.
C'MON. WE'RE OUTTA HERE FOR REAL THIS TIME.
OOOOOHHH... WHAT A RIDE!
THAT WAS JUST BRILLIANT!
...AND LOOK! NOW YOU'VE LET THEM GET AWAY!
ME?! I WAS DOING FINE UNTIL YOU CAME ALONG!
THAT'S WHAT YOU ALWAYS SAY. WE'VE GOT A REAL PROBLEM HERE.
YEAH...YOUR PITUITARY GLAND.
THIS CITY SIMPLY ISN'T BIG ENOUGH FOR TWO SUPER-HEROES...
...ONE OF US IS GOING TO HAVE TO GO.
AGREED!
OKAY, WELL...BYE BYE THEN.
ME?! NO WAY!

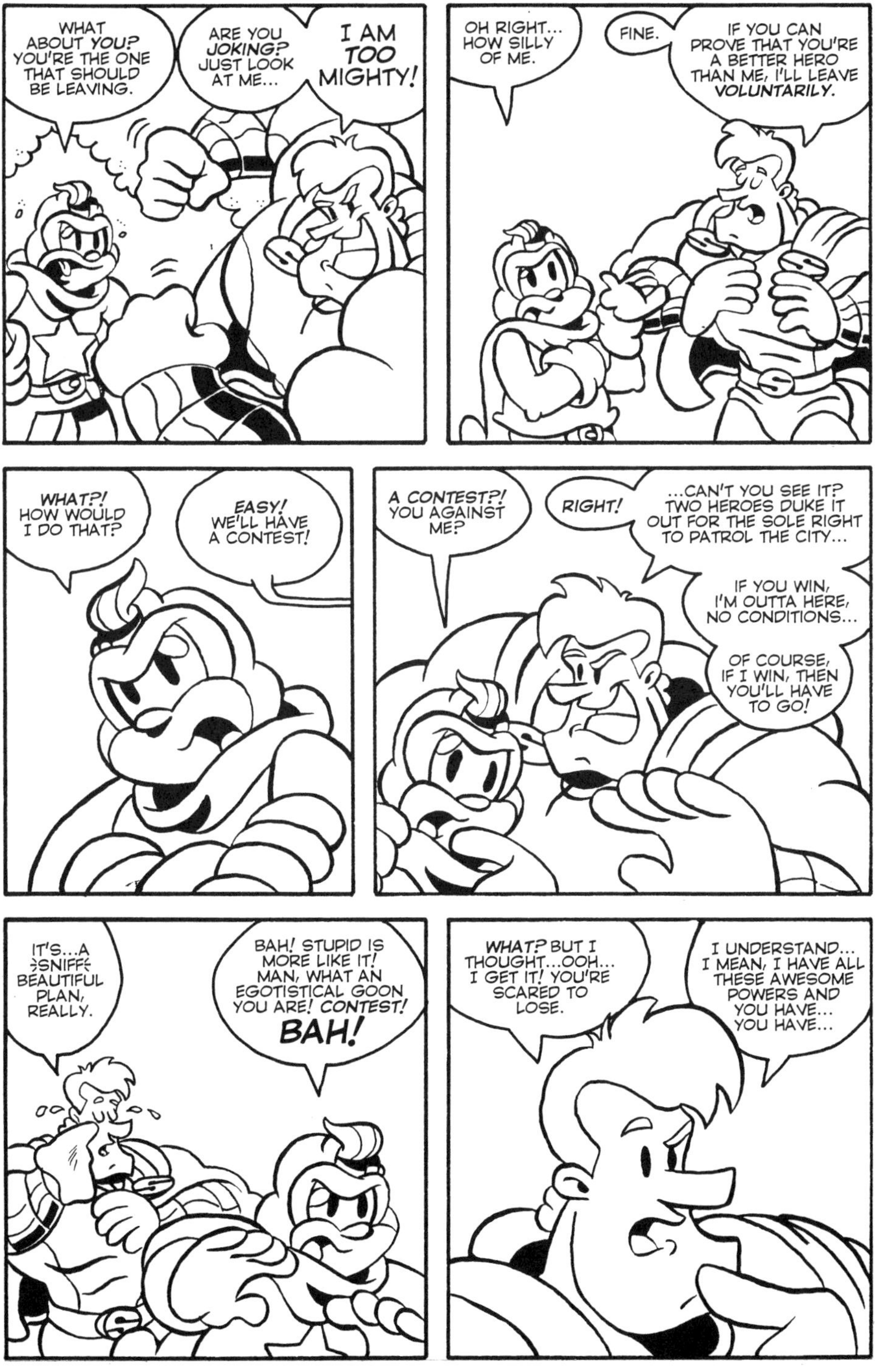
WHAT ABOUT *YOU?* YOU'RE THE ONE THAT SHOULD BE LEAVING.
ARE YOU *JOKING?* JUST LOOK AT ME...
I AM *TOO* MIGHTY!
OH RIGHT... HOW SILLY OF ME.
FINE.
IF YOU CAN PROVE THAT YOU'RE A BETTER HERO THAN ME, I'LL LEAVE ***VOLUNTARILY.***
WHAT?! HOW WOULD I DO THAT?
EASY! WE'LL HAVE A CONTEST!
A CONTEST?! YOU AGAINST ME?
RIGHT!
...CAN'T YOU SEE IT? TWO HEROES DUKE IT OUT FOR THE SOLE RIGHT TO PATROL THE CITY...
IF YOU WIN, I'M OUTTA HERE, NO CONDITIONS...
OF COURSE, IF I WIN, THEN YOU'LL HAVE TO GO!
IT'S...A SNIFF BEAUTIFUL PLAN, REALLY.
BAH! STUPID IS MORE LIKE IT! MAN, WHAT AN EGOTISTICAL GOON YOU ARE! *CONTEST!* ***BAH!***
WHAT? BUT I THOUGHT...OOH... I GET IT! YOU'RE SCARED TO LOSE.
I UNDERSTAND... I MEAN, I HAVE ALL THESE AWESOME POWERS AND YOU HAVE... YOU HAVE...

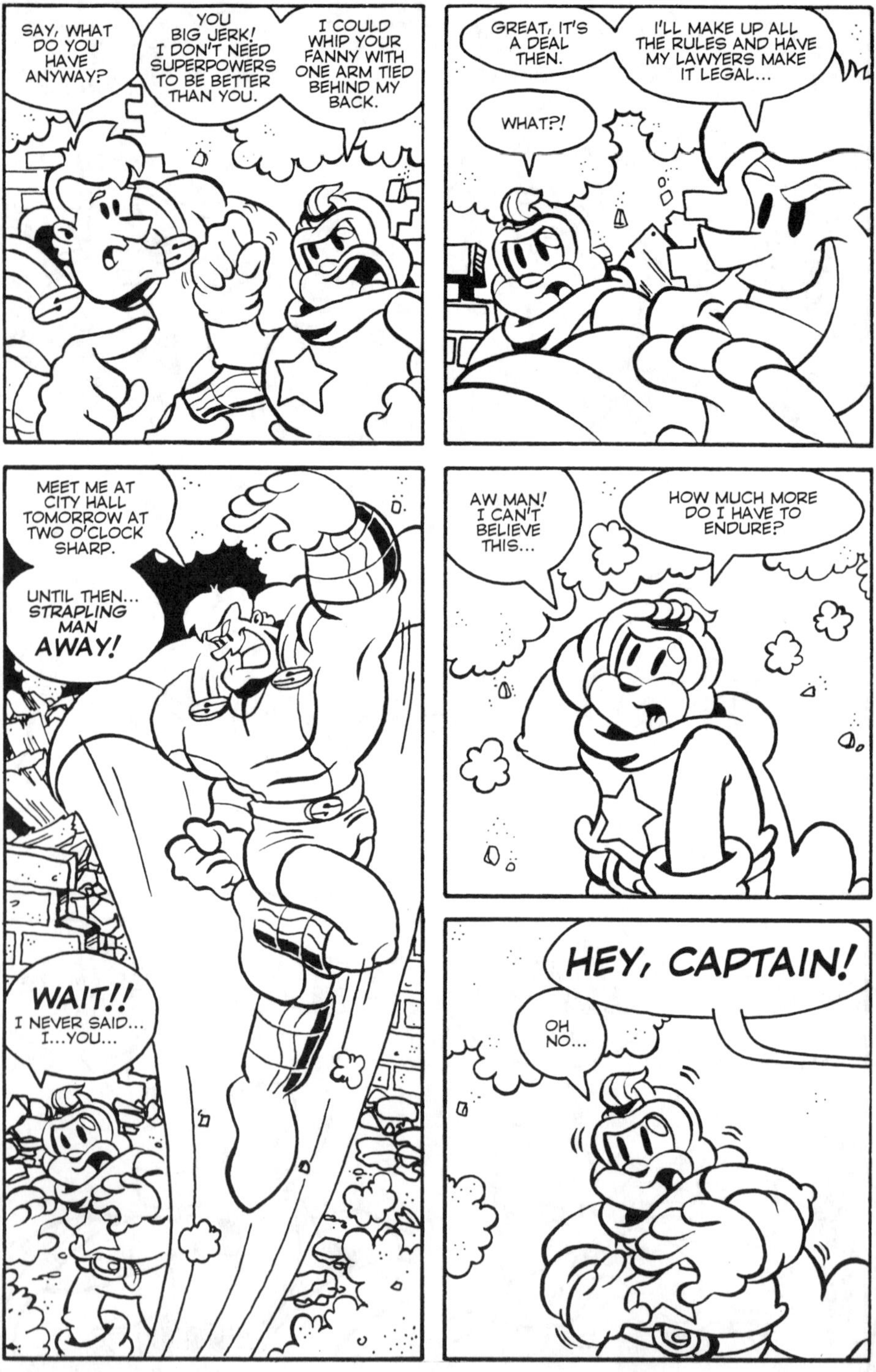
SAY, WHAT DO YOU HAVE ANYWAY?
YOU BIG JERK! I DON'T NEED SUPERPOWERS TO BE BETTER THAN YOU.
I COULD WHIP YOUR FANNY WITH ONE ARM TIED BEHIND MY BACK.
GREAT, IT'S A DEAL THEN.
I'LL MAKE UP ALL THE RULES AND HAVE MY LAWYERS MAKE IT LEGAL...
WHAT?!
MEET ME AT CITY HALL TOMORROW AT TWO O'CLOCK SHARP.
UNTIL THEN... STRAPLING MAN AWAY!
WAIT!! I NEVER SAID... I...YOU...
AW MAN! I CAN'T BELIEVE THIS...
HOW MUCH MORE DO I HAVE TO ENDURE?
HEY, CAPTAIN!
OH NO...

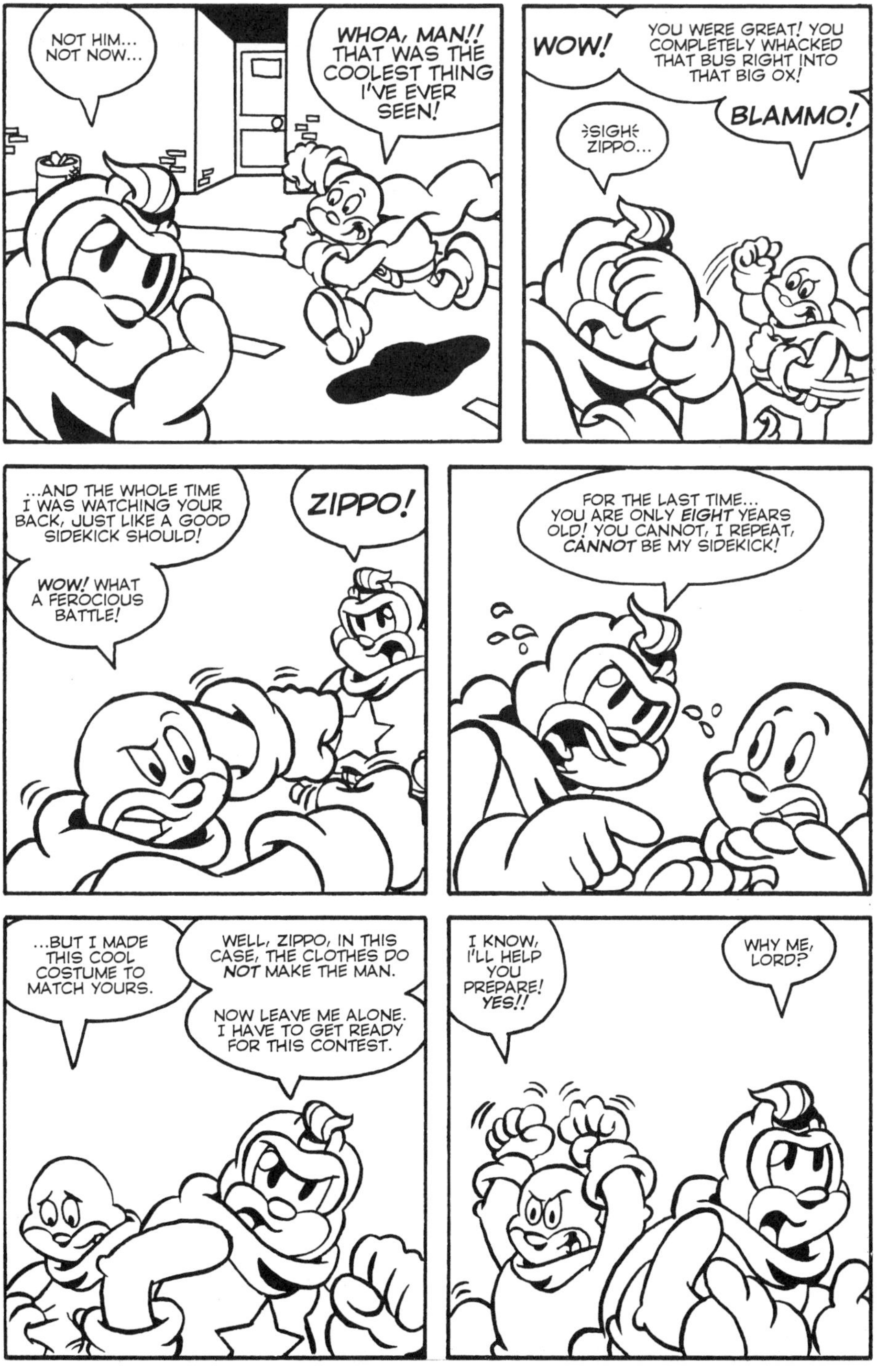
NOT HIM... NOT NOW...
WHOA, MAN!! THAT WAS THE COOLEST THING I'VE EVER SEEN!
WOW!
YOU WERE GREAT! YOU COMPLETELY WHACKED THAT BUS RIGHT INTO THAT BIG OX!
BLAMMO!
SIGH ZIPPO...
...AND THE WHOLE TIME I WAS WATCHING YOUR BACK, JUST LIKE A GOOD SIDEKICK SHOULD!
WOW! WHAT A FEROCIOUS BATTLE!
ZIPPO!
FOR THE LAST TIME... YOU ARE ONLY EIGHT YEARS OLD! YOU CANNOT, I REPEAT, CANNOT BE MY SIDEKICK!
...BUT I MADE THIS COOL COSTUME TO MATCH YOURS.
WELL, ZIPPO, IN THIS CASE, THE CLOTHES DO NOT MAKE THE MAN.
NOW LEAVE ME ALONE. I HAVE TO GET READY FOR THIS CONTEST.
I KNOW, I'LL HELP YOU PREPARE! YES!!
WHY ME, LORD?

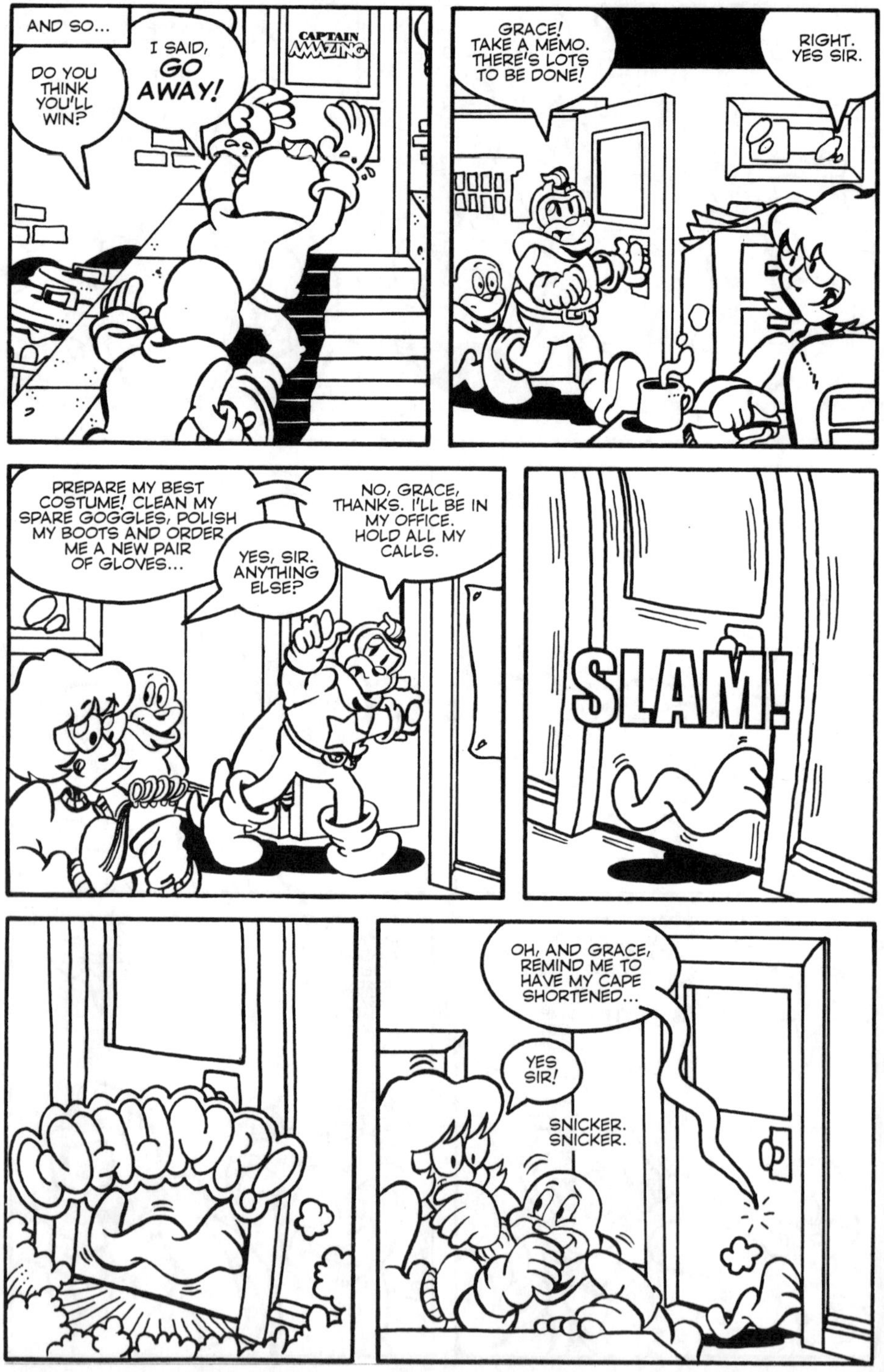
AND SO...
DO YOU THINK YOU'LL WIN?
I SAID, GO AWAY!
CAPTAIN AMAZING
GRACE! TAKE A MEMO. THERE'S LOTS TO BE DONE!
RIGHT. YES SIR.
PREPARE MY BEST COSTUME! CLEAN MY SPARE GOGGLES, POLISH MY BOOTS AND ORDER ME A NEW PAIR OF GLOVES...
YES, SIR. ANYTHING ELSE?
NO, GRACE, THANKS. I'LL BE IN MY OFFICE. HOLD ALL MY CALLS.
SLAM!
WHUMP!
OH, AND GRACE, REMIND ME TO HAVE MY CAPE SHORTENED...
YES SIR!
SNICKER. SNICKER.

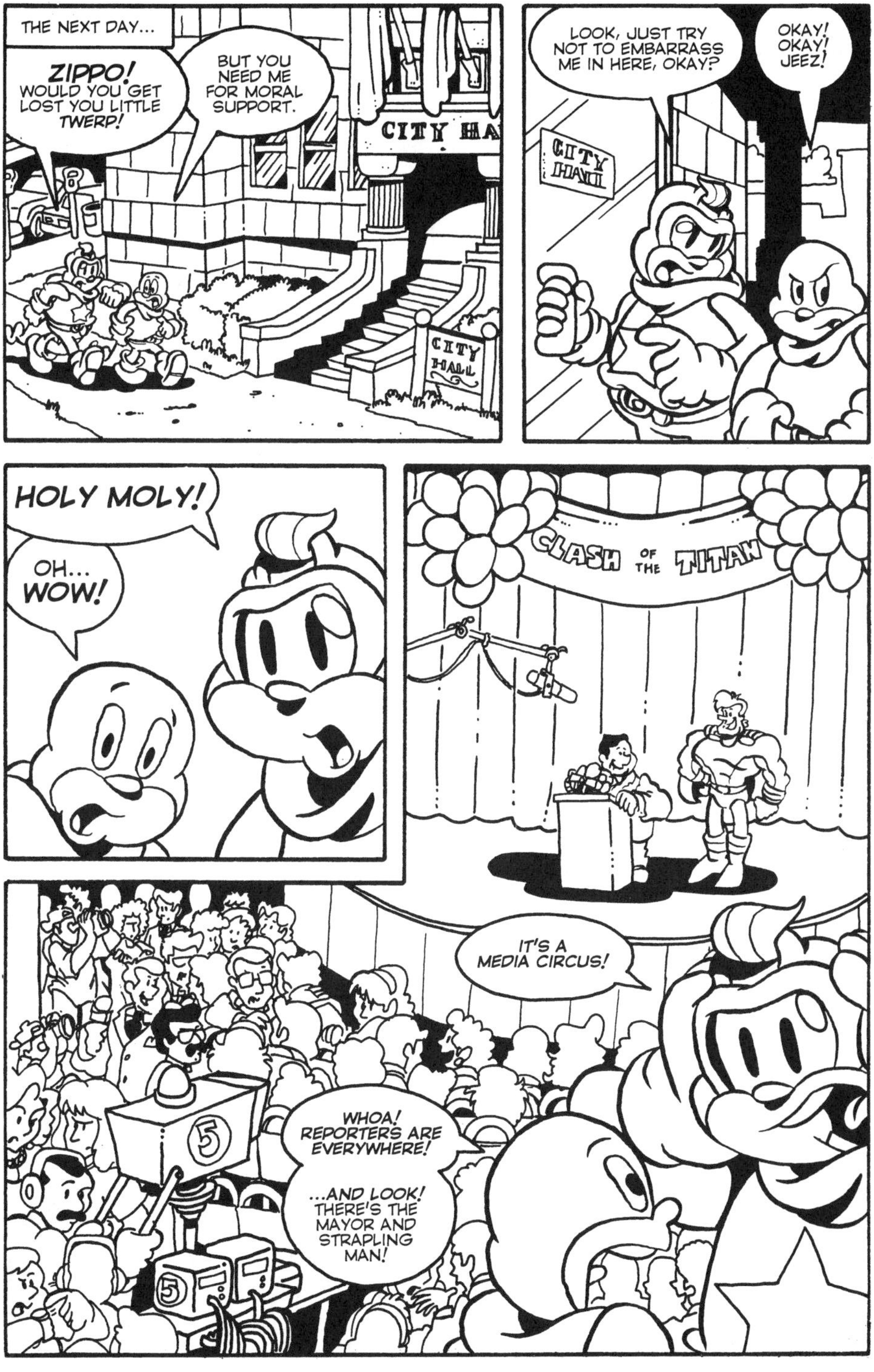

THE NEXT DAY...
ZIPPO! WOULD YOU GET LOST YOU LITTLE TWERP!
BUT YOU NEED ME FOR MORAL SUPPORT.
CITY HALL
CITY HALL
LOOK, JUST TRY NOT TO EMBARRASS ME IN HERE, OKAY?
OKAY! OKAY! JEEZ!
CITY HALL
HOLY MOLY!
OH... WOW!
CLASH OF THE TITAN
IT'S A MEDIA CIRCUS!
WHOA! REPORTERS ARE EVERYWHERE!
...AND LOOK! THERE'S THE MAYOR AND STRAPLING MAN!

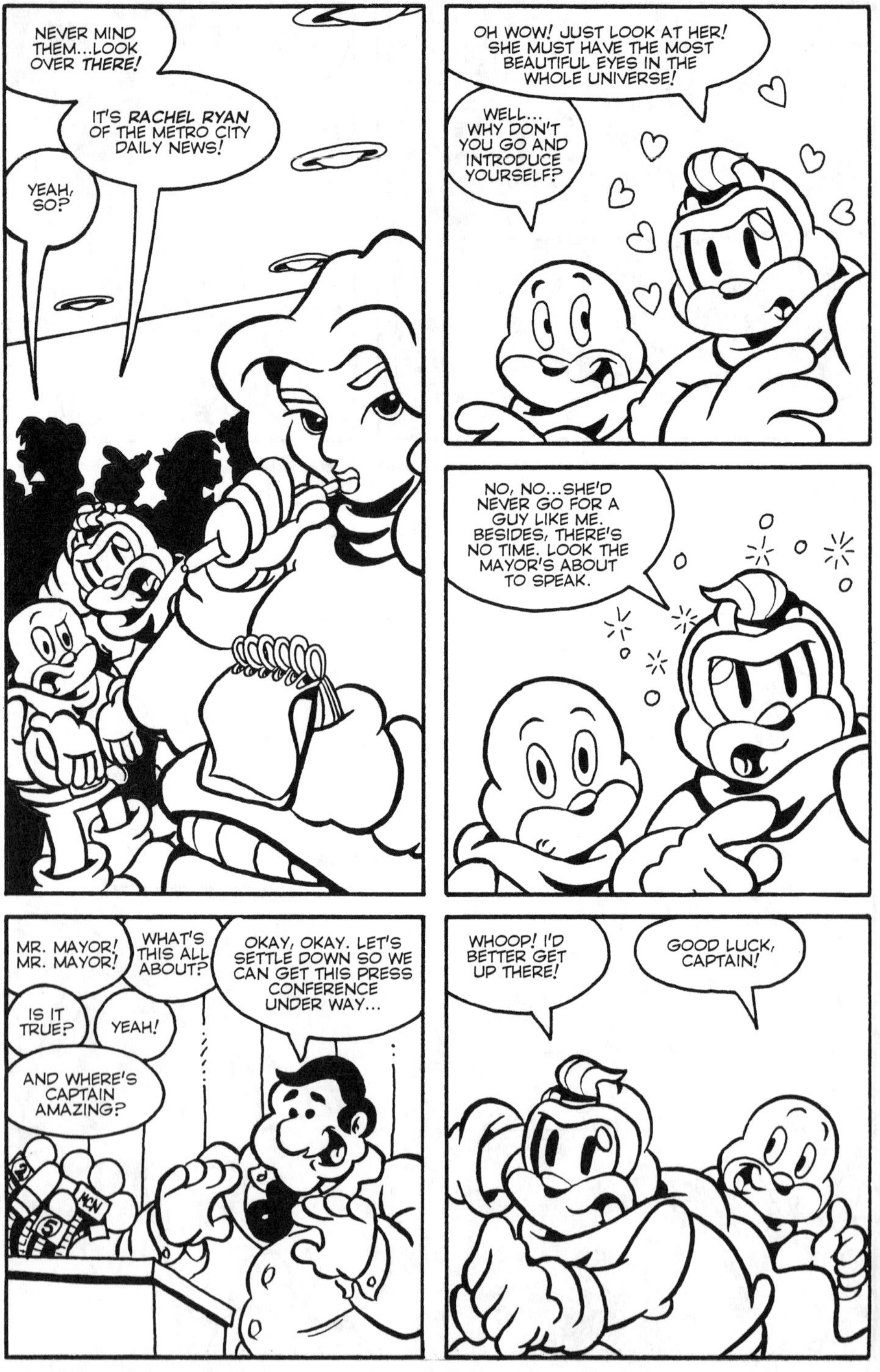
NEVER MIND THEM...LOOK OVER THERE!
IT'S RACHEL RYAN OF THE METRO CITY DAILY NEWS!
YEAH, SO?
OH WOW! JUST LOOK AT HER! SHE MUST HAVE THE MOST BEAUTIFUL EYES IN THE WHOLE UNIVERSE!
WELL... WHY DON'T YOU GO AND INTRODUCE YOURSELF?
NO, NO...SHE'D NEVER GO FOR A GUY LIKE ME. BESIDES, THERE'S NO TIME. LOOK THE MAYOR'S ABOUT TO SPEAK.
MR. MAYOR! MR. MAYOR!
WHAT'S THIS ALL ABOUT?
IS IT TRUE?
YEAH!
AND WHERE'S CAPTAIN AMAZING?
OKAY, OKAY. LET'S SETTLE DOWN SO WE CAN GET THIS PRESS CONFERENCE UNDER WAY...
WHOOP! I'D BETTER GET UP THERE!
GOOD LUCK, CAPTAIN!

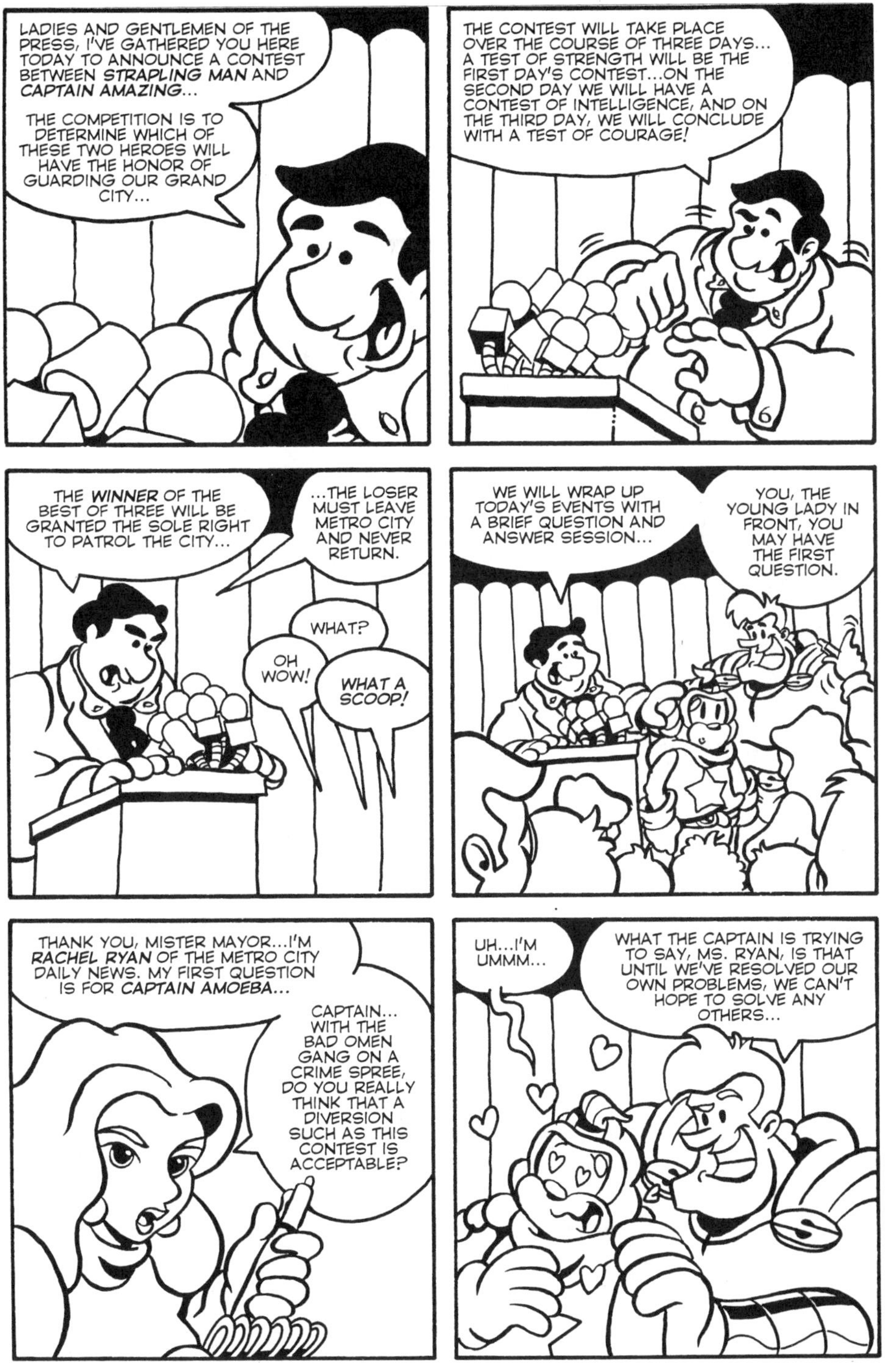
LADIES AND GENTLEMEN OF THE PRESS, I'VE GATHERED YOU HERE TODAY TO ANNOUNCE A CONTEST BETWEEN STRAPLING MAN AND CAPTAIN AMAZING...
THE COMPETITION IS TO DETERMINE WHICH OF THESE TWO HEROES WILL HAVE THE HONOR OF GUARDING OUR GRAND CITY...
THE CONTEST WILL TAKE PLACE OVER THE COURSE OF THREE DAYS... A TEST OF STRENGTH WILL BE THE FIRST DAY'S CONTEST...ON THE SECOND DAY WE WILL HAVE A CONTEST OF INTELLIGENCE, AND ON THE THIRD DAY, WE WILL CONCLUDE WITH A TEST OF COURAGE!
THE WINNER OF THE BEST OF THREE WILL BE GRANTED THE SOLE RIGHT TO PATROL THE CITY...
...THE LOSER MUST LEAVE METRO CITY AND NEVER RETURN.
WHAT?
OH WOW!
WHAT A SCOOP!
WE WILL WRAP UP TODAY'S EVENTS WITH A BRIEF QUESTION AND ANSWER SESSION...
YOU, THE YOUNG LADY IN FRONT, YOU MAY HAVE THE FIRST QUESTION.
THANK YOU, MISTER MAYOR...I'M RACHEL RYAN OF THE METRO CITY DAILY NEWS. MY FIRST QUESTION IS FOR CAPTAIN AMOEBA...
CAPTAIN... WITH THE BAD OMEN GANG ON A CRIME SPREE, DO YOU REALLY THINK THAT A DIVERSION SUCH AS THIS CONTEST IS ACCEPTABLE?
UH...I'M UMMM...
WHAT THE CAPTAIN IS TRYING TO SAY, MS. RYAN, IS THAT UNTIL WE'VE RESOLVED OUR OWN PROBLEMS, WE CAN'T HOPE TO SOLVE ANY OTHERS...

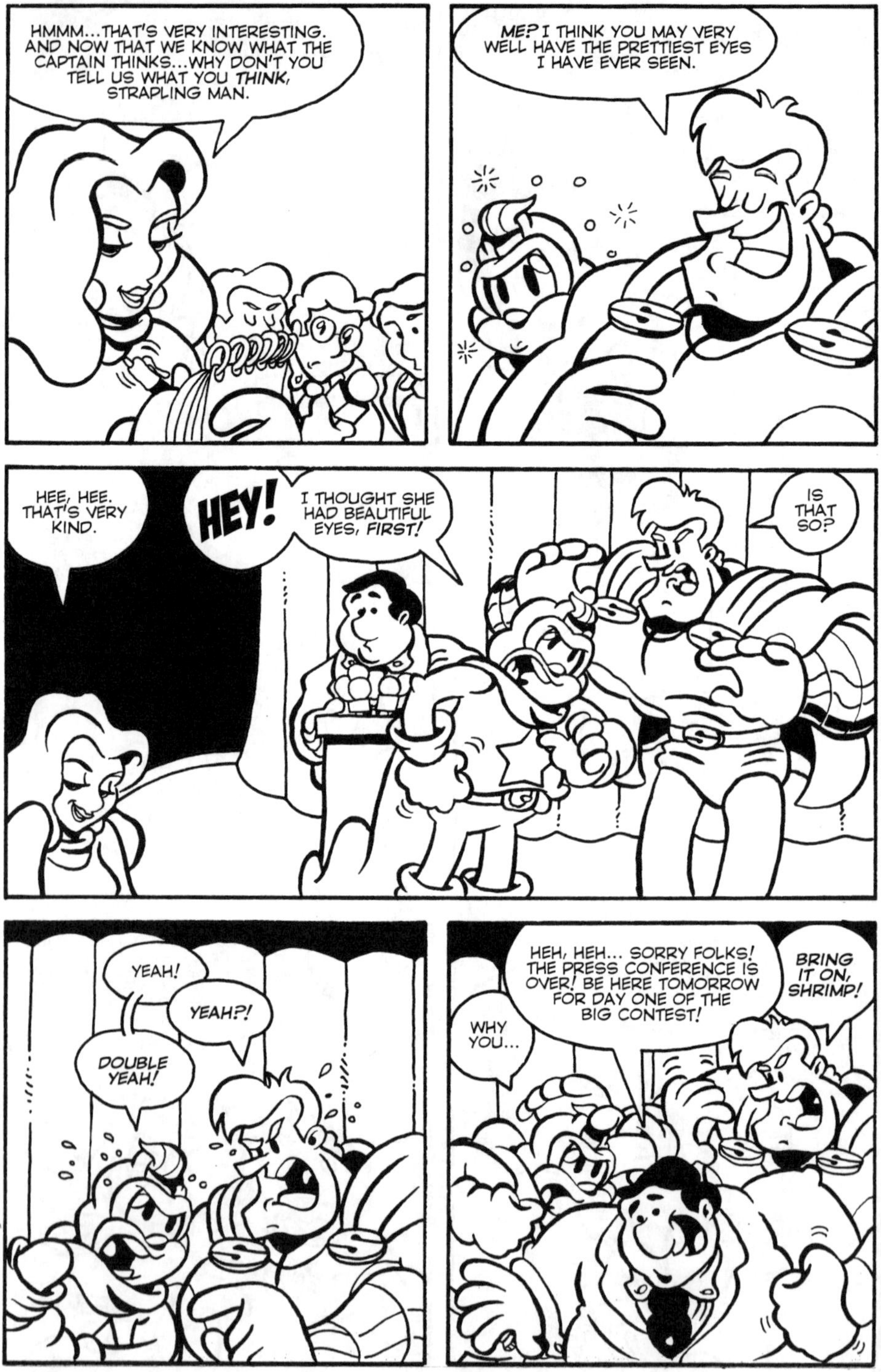
HMMM...THAT'S VERY INTERESTING. AND NOW THAT WE KNOW WHAT THE CAPTAIN THINKS...WHY DON'T YOU TELL US WHAT YOU THINK, STRAPLING MAN.
ME? I THINK YOU MAY VERY WELL HAVE THE PRETTIEST EYES I HAVE EVER SEEN.
HEE, HEE. THAT'S VERY KIND.
HEY!
I THOUGHT SHE HAD BEAUTIFUL EYES, FIRST!
IS THAT SO?
YEAH!
YEAH?!
DOUBLE YEAH!
WHY YOU...
HEH, HEH... SORRY FOLKS! THE PRESS CONFERENCE IS OVER! BE HERE TOMORROW FOR DAY ONE OF THE BIG CONTEST!
BRING IT ON, SHRIMP!

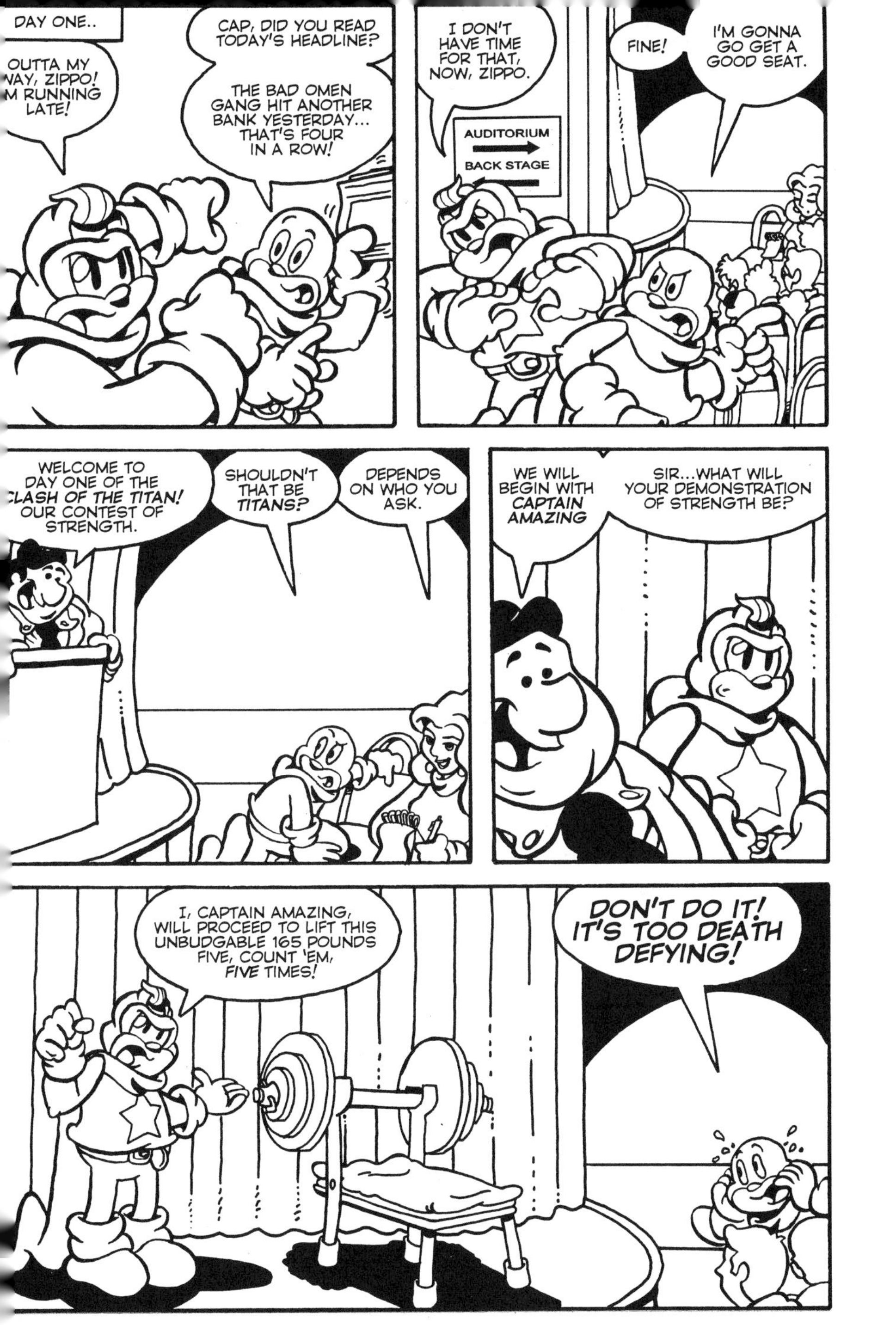
DAY ONE..
OUTTA MY WAY, ZIPPO! M RUNNING LATE!
CAP, DID YOU READ TODAY'S HEADLINE?
THE BAD OMEN GANG HIT ANOTHER BANK YESTERDAY... THAT'S FOUR IN A ROW!
I DON'T HAVE TIME FOR THAT, NOW, ZIPPO.
AUDITORIUM
BACK STAGE
FINE!
I'M GONNA GO GET A GOOD SEAT.
WELCOME TO DAY ONE OF THE CLASH OF THE TITAN! OUR CONTEST OF STRENGTH.
SHOULDN'T THAT BE TITANS?
DEPENDS ON WHO YOU ASK.
WE WILL BEGIN WITH CAPTAIN AMAZING
SIR...WHAT WILL YOUR DEMONSTRATION OF STRENGTH BE?
I, CAPTAIN AMAZING, WILL PROCEED TO LIFT THIS UNBUDGABLE 165 POUNDS FIVE, COUNT 'EM, FIVE TIMES!
DON'T DO IT! IT'S TOO DEATH DEFYING!

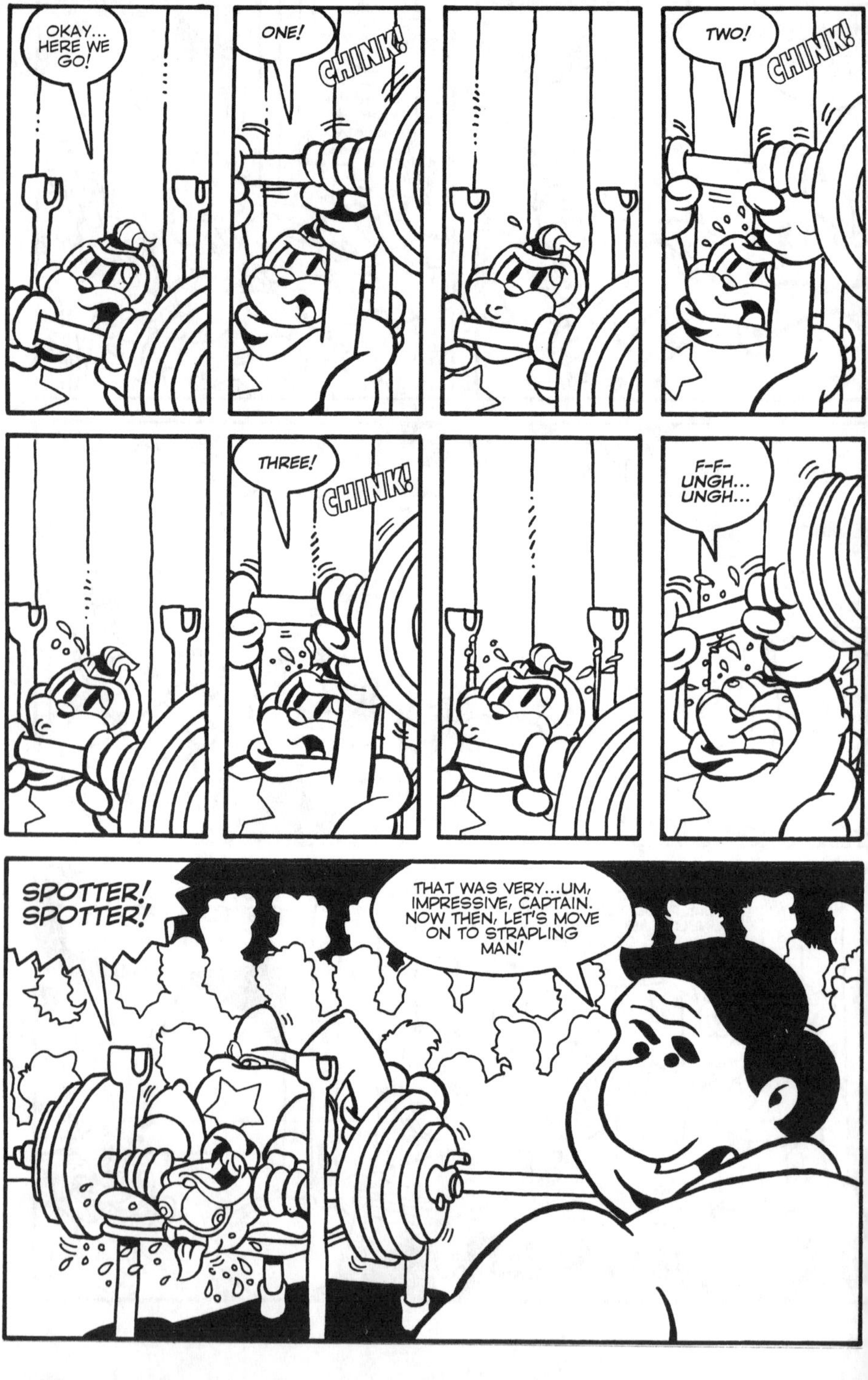
OKAY... HERE WE GO!
ONE!
CHINK!
TWO!
CHINK!
THREE!
CHINK!
F-F- UNGH... UNGH...
SPOTTER! SPOTTER!
THAT WAS VERY...UM, IMPRESSIVE, CAPTAIN. NOW THEN, LET'S MOVE ON TO STRAPLING MAN!

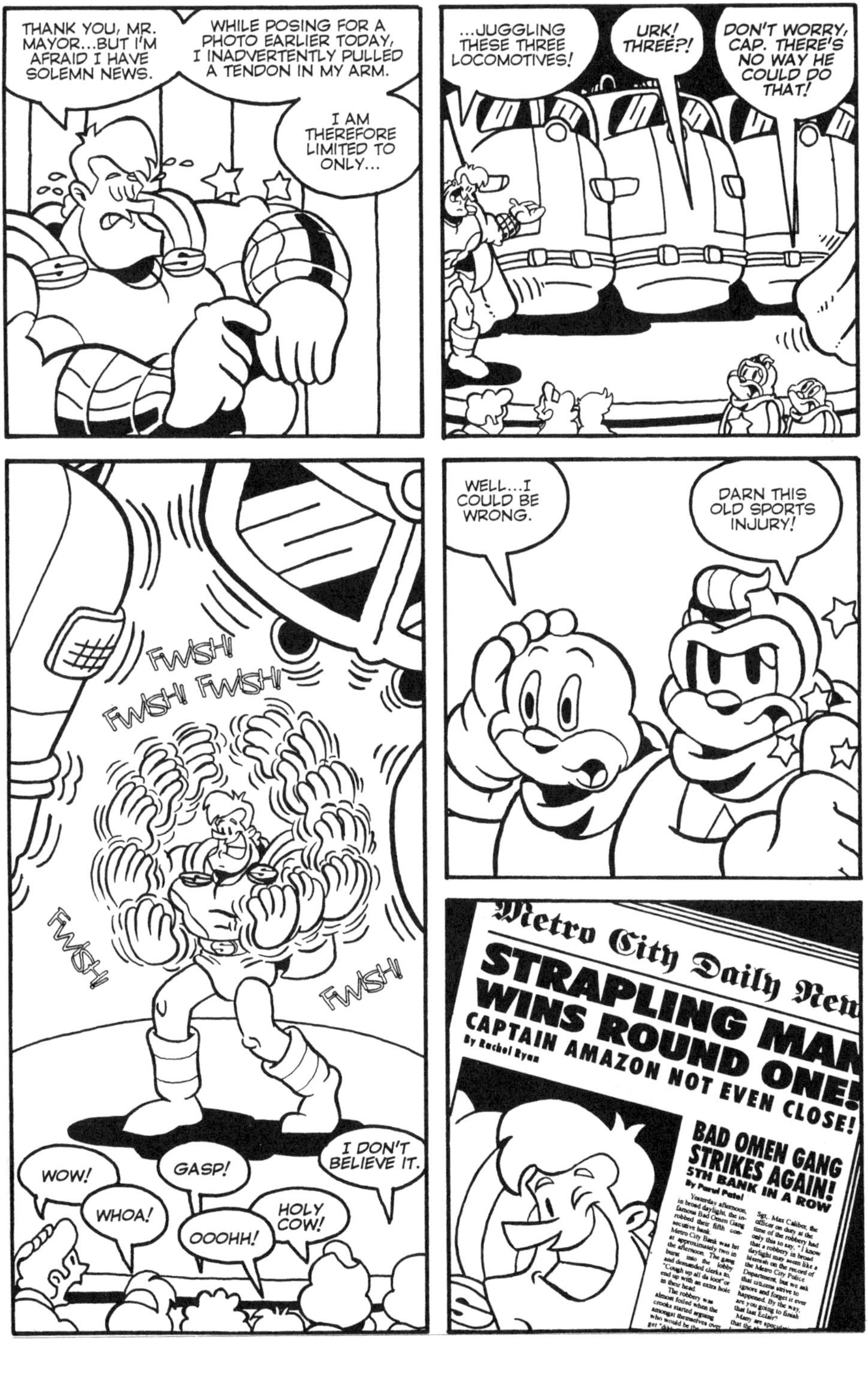
THANK YOU, MR. MAYOR...BUT I'M AFRAID I HAVE SOLEMN NEWS.
WHILE POSING FOR A PHOTO EARLIER TODAY, I INADVERTENTLY PULLED A TENDON IN MY ARM.
I AM THEREFORE LIMITED TO ONLY...
...JUGGLING THESE THREE LOCOMOTIVES!
URK! THREE?!
DON'T WORRY, CAP. THERE'S NO WAY HE COULD DO THAT!
FWISH!
FWISH! FWISH!
FWISH!
FWISH!
FWISH!
WOW!
WHOA!
GASP!
OOOHH!
HOLY COW!
I DON'T BELIEVE IT.
WELL...I COULD BE WRONG.
DARN THIS OLD SPORTS INJURY!
Metro City Daily New
STRAPLING MAN WINS ROUND ONE!
CAPTAIN AMAZON NOT EVEN CLOSE!
By Rachel Ryan
BAD OMEN GANG STRIKES AGAIN!
5TH BANK IN A ROW
By Parul Patel
Yesterday afternoon, in broad daylight, the infamous Bad Omen Gang robbed their fifth consecutive bank.
Metro City Bank was hit at approximately two in the afternoon. The gang burst into the lobby and demanded clerks to, "Cough up all da loot" or end up with an extra hole in their head.
The robbery was almost foiled when the crooks started arguing amongst themselves over who would be the
Sgt.. Max Caliber, the officer on duty at the time of the robbery had only this to say, "I know that a robbery in broad daylight may seem like a blemish on the record of the Metro City Police Department, but we ask that citizens strive to ignore and forget it ever happened. By the way, are you going to finish that last Eclair?"

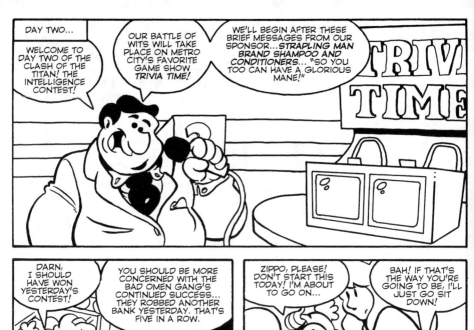

DAY TWO...

WELCOME TO DAY TWO OF THE CLASH OF THE TITAN! THE INTELLIGENCE CONTEST!

OUR BATTLE OF WITS WILL TAKE PLACE ON METRO CITY'S FAVORITE GAME SHOW *TRIVIA TIME!*

WE'LL BEGIN AFTER THESE BRIEF MESSAGES FROM OUR SPONSOR...*STRAPLING MAN BRAND SHAMPOO AND CONDITIONERS...* "SO YOU TOO CAN HAVE A GLORIOUS MANE!"

TRIVIA TIME

DARN, I SHOULD HAVE WON YESTERDAY'S CONTEST!

YOU SHOULD BE MORE CONCERNED WITH THE BAD OMEN GANG'S CONTINUED SUCCESS... THEY ROBBED ANOTHER BANK YESTERDAY. THAT'S FIVE IN A ROW.

ZIPPO, PLEASE! DON'T START THIS TODAY! I'M ABOUT TO GO ON...

BAH! IF THAT'S THE WAY YOU'RE GOING TO BE, I'LL JUST GO SIT DOWN!

CAPTAIN AMUSING

HI, RACHEL! DO YOU MIND IF I SIT NEXT TO YOU AGAIN TODAY?

NO! OF COURSE NOT. UM...WHAT IS YOUR NAME AGAIN, SWEETIE?

ZIPPO! I'M THE CAPTAIN'S SIDEKICK!

REALLY?! I DIDN'T KNOW HE HAD ONE...

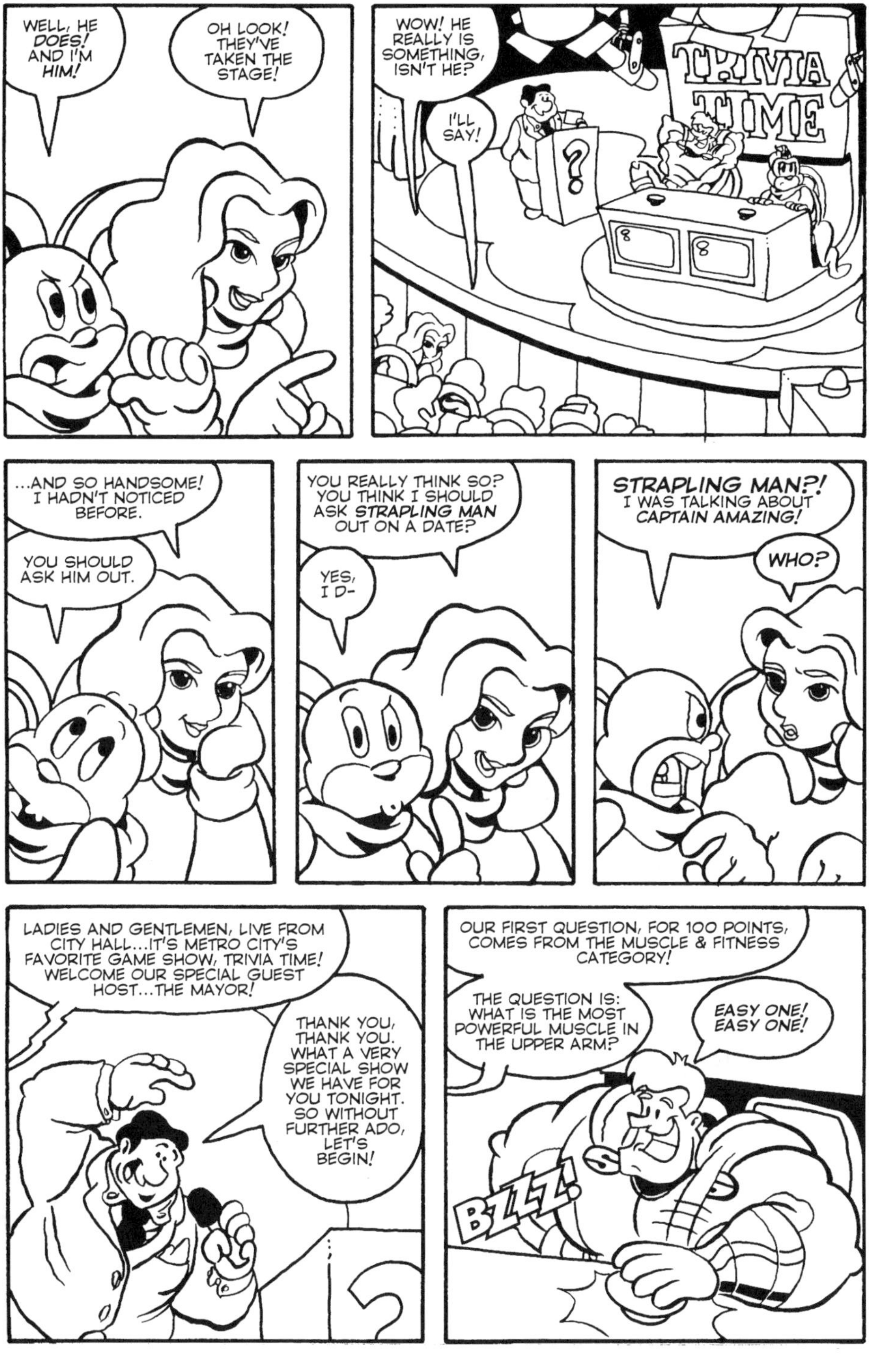

WELL, HE DOES! AND I'M HIM!
OH LOOK! THEY'VE TAKEN THE STAGE!
WOW! HE REALLY IS SOMETHING, ISN'T HE?
I'LL SAY!
TRIVIA TIME
...AND SO HANDSOME! I HADN'T NOTICED BEFORE.
YOU SHOULD ASK HIM OUT.
YOU REALLY THINK SO? YOU THINK I SHOULD ASK STRAPLING MAN OUT ON A DATE?
YES, I D-
STRAPLING MAN?! I WAS TALKING ABOUT CAPTAIN AMAZING!
WHO?
LADIES AND GENTLEMEN, LIVE FROM CITY HALL...IT'S METRO CITY'S FAVORITE GAME SHOW, TRIVIA TIME! WELCOME OUR SPECIAL GUEST HOST...THE MAYOR!
THANK YOU, THANK YOU. WHAT A VERY SPECIAL SHOW WE HAVE FOR YOU TONIGHT. SO WITHOUT FURTHER ADO, LET'S BEGIN!
OUR FIRST QUESTION, FOR 100 POINTS, COMES FROM THE MUSCLE & FITNESS CATEGORY!
THE QUESTION IS: WHAT IS THE MOST POWERFUL MUSCLE IN THE UPPER ARM?
EASY ONE! EASY ONE!
BZZZ!

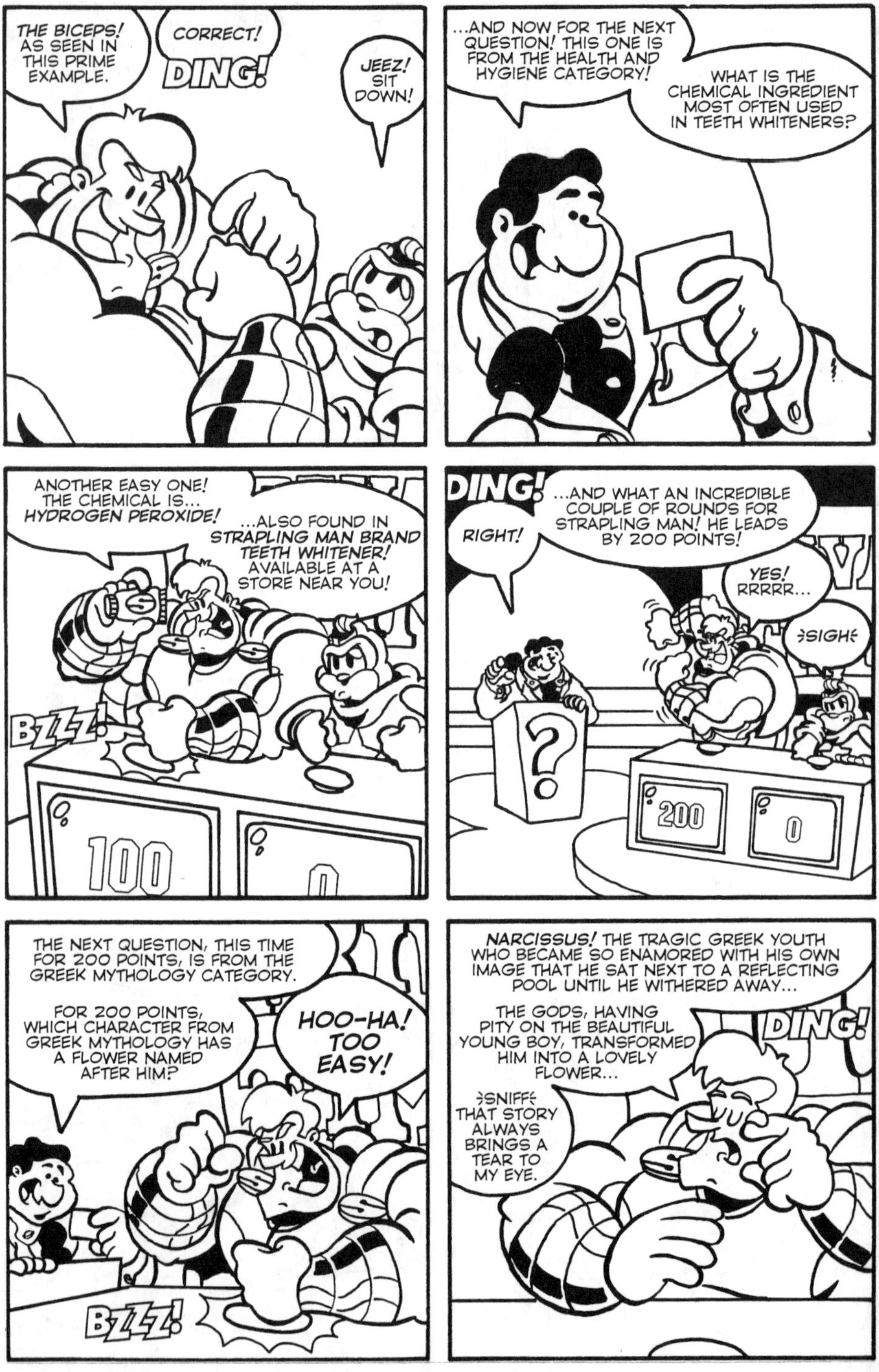
THE BICEPS! AS SEEN IN THIS PRIME EXAMPLE.
CORRECT!
DING!
JEEZ! SIT DOWN!
...AND NOW FOR THE NEXT QUESTION! THIS ONE IS FROM THE HEALTH AND HYGIENE CATEGORY!
WHAT IS THE CHEMICAL INGREDIENT MOST OFTEN USED IN TEETH WHITENERS?
ANOTHER EASY ONE! THE CHEMICAL IS... HYDROGEN PEROXIDE!
...ALSO FOUND IN STRAPLING MAN BRAND TEETH WHITENER! AVAILABLE AT A STORE NEAR YOU!
BZZZ!
100
0
DING!
RIGHT!
...AND WHAT AN INCREDIBLE COUPLE OF ROUNDS FOR STRAPLING MAN! HE LEADS BY 200 POINTS!
YES! RRRRR...
SIGH
200
0
THE NEXT QUESTION, THIS TIME FOR 200 POINTS, IS FROM THE GREEK MYTHOLOGY CATEGORY.
FOR 200 POINTS, WHICH CHARACTER FROM GREEK MYTHOLOGY HAS A FLOWER NAMED AFTER HIM?
HOO-HA! TOO EASY!
BZZZ!
NARCISSUS! THE TRAGIC GREEK YOUTH WHO BECAME SO ENAMORED WITH HIS OWN IMAGE THAT HE SAT NEXT TO A REFLECTING POOL UNTIL HE WITHERED AWAY...
THE GODS, HAVING PITY ON THE BEAUTIFUL YOUNG BOY, TRANSFORMED HIM INTO A LOVELY FLOWER...
DING!
SNIFF THAT STORY ALWAYS BRINGS A TEAR TO MY EYE.

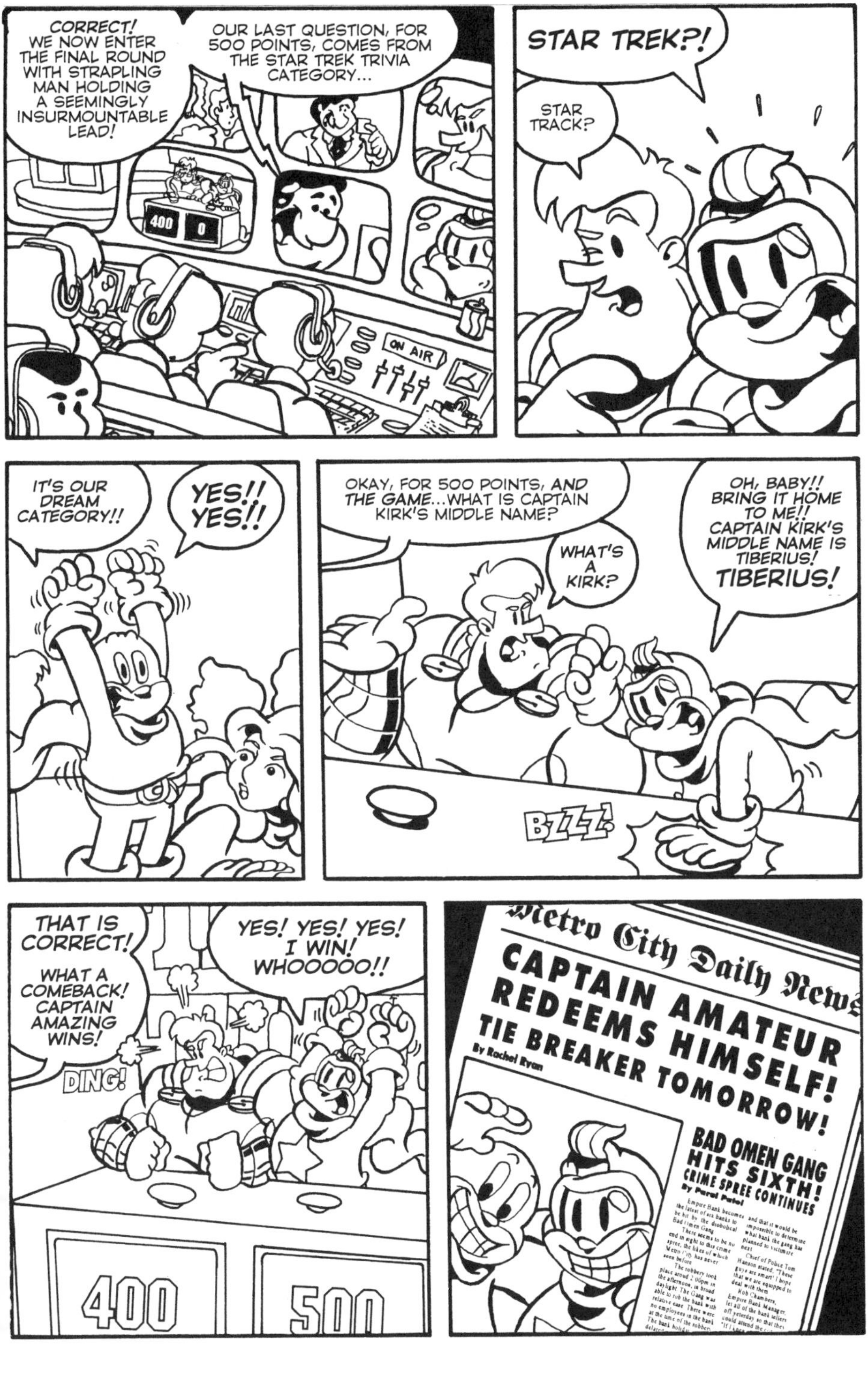

CORRECT! WE NOW ENTER THE FINAL ROUND WITH STRAPLING MAN HOLDING A SEEMINGLY INSURMOUNTABLE LEAD!
OUR LAST QUESTION, FOR 500 POINTS, COMES FROM THE STAR TREK TRIVIA CATEGORY...
400
0
ON AIR
STAR TREK?!
STAR TRACK?
IT'S OUR DREAM CATEGORY!!
YES!! YES!!
OKAY, FOR 500 POINTS, AND THE GAME...WHAT IS CAPTAIN KIRK'S MIDDLE NAME?
WHAT'S A KIRK?
OH, BABY!! BRING IT HOME TO ME!! CAPTAIN KIRK'S MIDDLE NAME IS TIBERIUS! TIBERIUS!
BZZZ!
THAT IS CORRECT!
WHAT A COMEBACK! CAPTAIN AMAZING WINS!
DING!
YES! YES! YES! I WIN! WHOOOOO!!
400
500
Metro City Daily News
CAPTAIN AMATEUR REDEEMS HIMSELF! TIE BREAKER TOMORROW!
By Rachel Ryan
BAD OMEN GANG HITS SIXTH! CRIME SPREE CONTINUES
By Parul Patel
Empire Bank becomes the latest of six banks to be hit by the diobolical Bad Omen Gang.
There seems to be no end in sight to this crime spree, the likes of which Metro City has never seen before.
The robbery took place aroud 2:00pm in the afternoon, in broad daylight. The Gang was able to rob the bank with relative ease. There were no employees in the bank at the time of the robbery.
and that it would be impossible to determine what bank the gang has planned to victimize next.
Chief of Police Tom Hanson stated, "These guys are smart! I hope that we are equipped to deal with them.
Rob Chambers, Empire Bank Manager, let all of the bank tellers off yeterday so that they could attend the

DAY THREE...

I'VE GOT TO FIGURE OUT A WAY TO WIN TODAY! WHAT CAN I DO? WHAT CAN I DO?

CAP! CAP! I NEED YOUR HELP ANALYZING THIS DATA I GATHERED ON THE BAD OMEN GANG'S CRIME SPREE!

NOT THAT AGAIN. ZIPPO, RUN ALONG... I'M BUSY NOW.

BUSY?!

I HAVE TO GET READY FOR THE CONTEST...

MAN, I THOUGHT YOU WERE A HERO, BUT YOU'RE JUST A BIG JERK!

YOU STINK!

≷SNIFF≷ THAT BIG JERK! I DIDN'T WANNA BE HIS STUPID SIDEKICK ANYWAY...

PROBLEMS, SHORT STUFF?

NEW

≷SNIFF≷ I'M WORKING ON A CASE AND NO ONE WILL HELP ME.

ON A CASE, HUH? WELL, LET ME SEE WHAT YOU HAVE SO FAR...

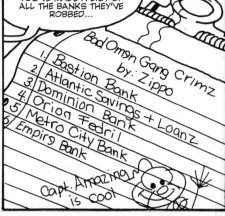

"BAD OMEN GANG CRIMES." YOU'VE MADE A LIST OF ALL THE BANKS THEY'VE ROBBED...

Bad Omen Gang Crimz by: Zippo

1. Bastion Bank
2. Atlantic Savings + Loanz
3. Dominion Bank
4. Orion Fedril
5. Metro City Bank
6. Empire Bank

Capt. Amazing is cool

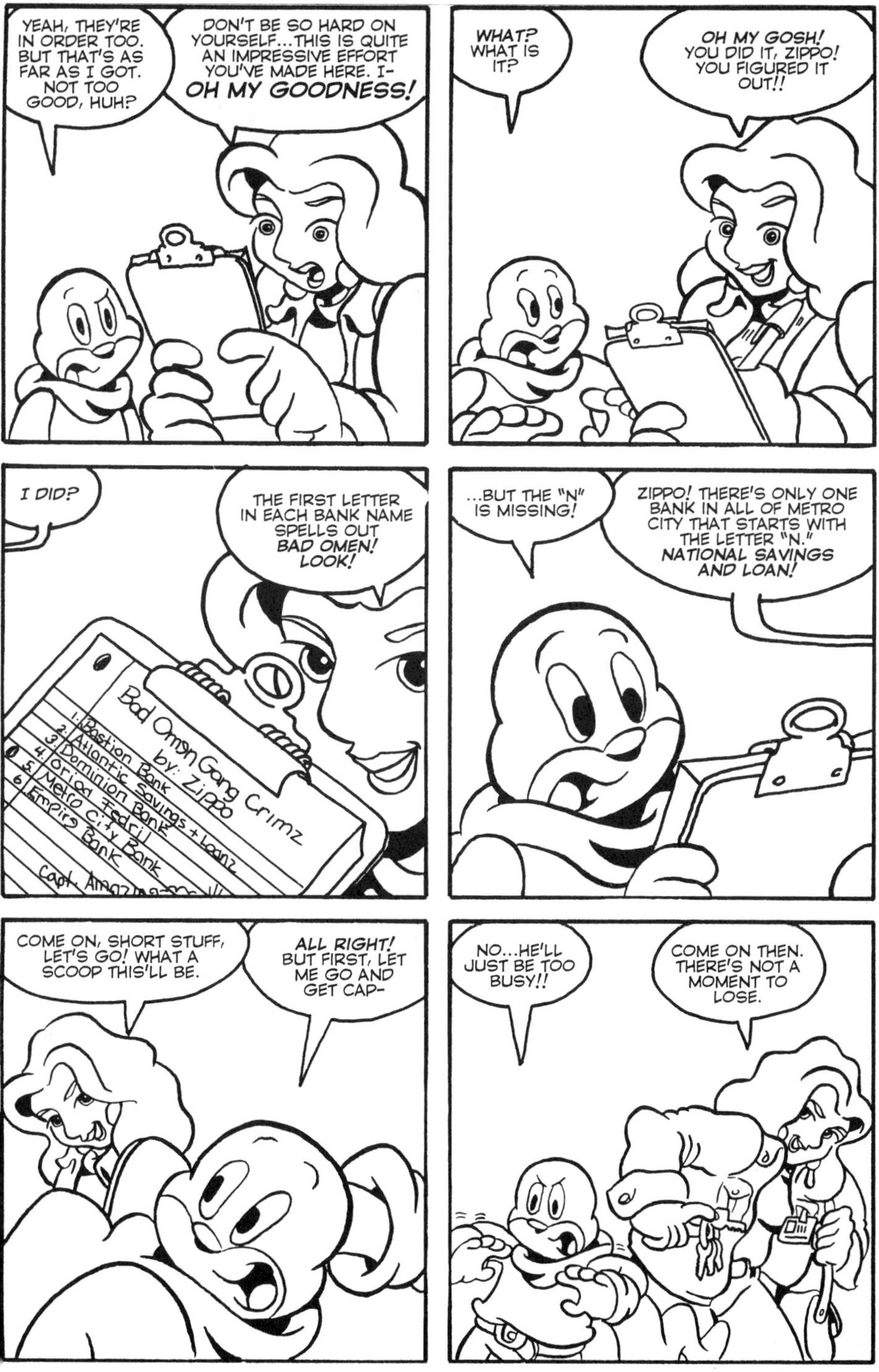

YEAH, THEY'RE IN ORDER TOO. BUT THAT'S AS FAR AS I GOT. NOT TOO GOOD, HUH?
DON'T BE SO HARD ON YOURSELF...THIS IS QUITE AN IMPRESSIVE EFFORT YOU'VE MADE HERE. I- OH MY GOODNESS!
WHAT? WHAT IS IT?
OH MY GOSH! YOU DID IT, ZIPPO! YOU FIGURED IT OUT!!
I DID?
THE FIRST LETTER IN EACH BANK NAME SPELLS OUT BAD OMEN! LOOK!
Bad Omen Gang Crimz
by: Zippo
1. Bastion Bank
2. Atlantic Bank
3. Dominion Savings + Loanz
4. Orion Fedril
5. Metro City Bank
6. Empire Bank
...BUT THE "N" IS MISSING!
ZIPPO! THERE'S ONLY ONE BANK IN ALL OF METRO CITY THAT STARTS WITH THE LETTER "N." NATIONAL SAVINGS AND LOAN!
COME ON, SHORT STUFF, LET'S GO! WHAT A SCOOP THIS'LL BE.
ALL RIGHT! BUT FIRST, LET ME GO AND GET CAP-
NO...HE'LL JUST BE TOO BUSY!!
COME ON THEN. THERE'S NOT A MOMENT TO LOSE.

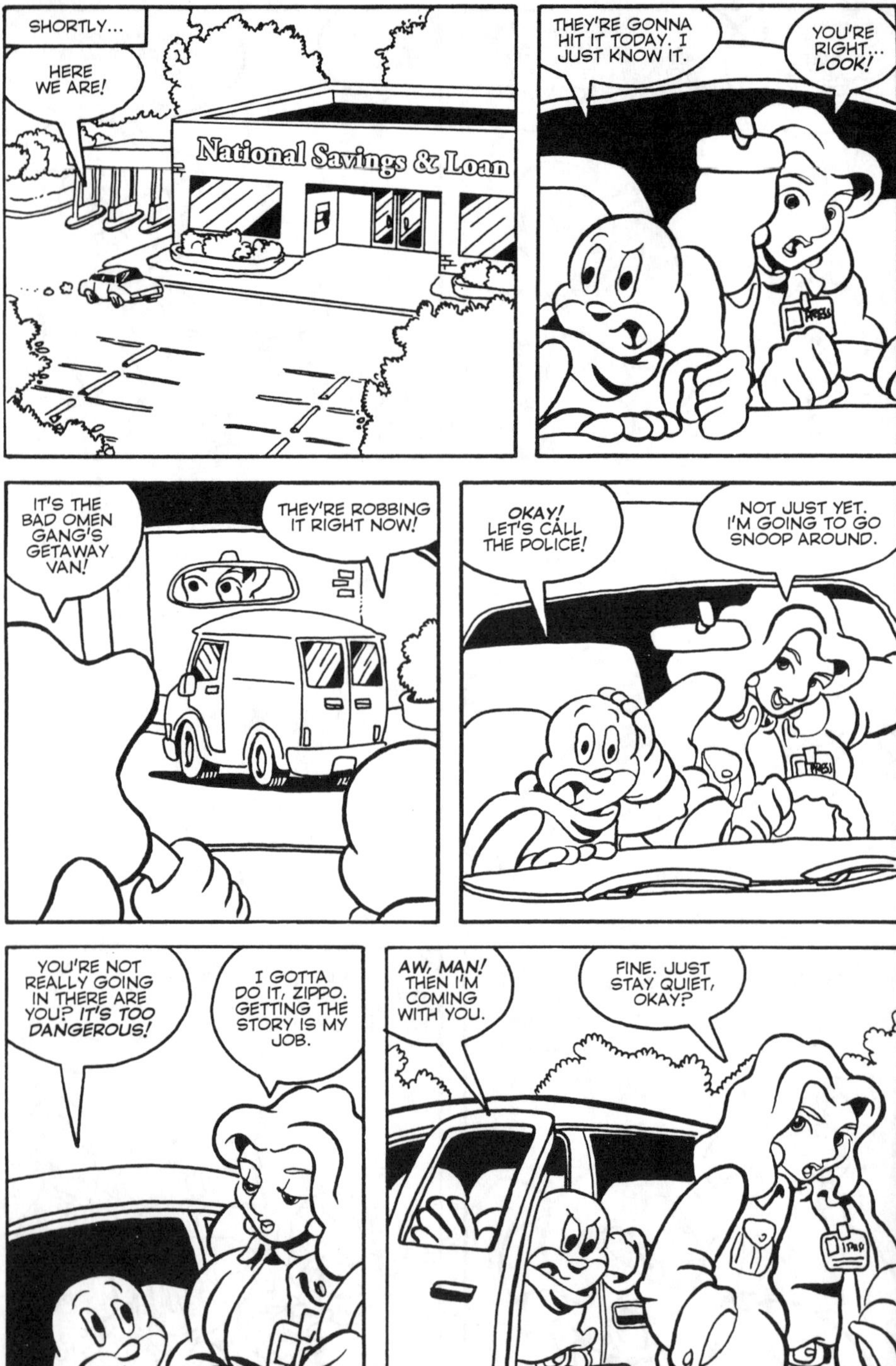
SHORTLY...
HERE WE ARE!
National Savings & Loan
THEY'RE GONNA HIT IT TODAY. I JUST KNOW IT.
YOU'RE RIGHT... LOOK!
IT'S THE BAD OMEN GANG'S GETAWAY VAN!
THEY'RE ROBBING IT RIGHT NOW!
OKAY! LET'S CALL THE POLICE!
NOT JUST YET. I'M GOING TO GO SNOOP AROUND.
YOU'RE NOT REALLY GOING IN THERE ARE YOU? IT'S TOO DANGEROUS!
I GOTTA DO IT, ZIPPO. GETTING THE STORY IS MY JOB.
AW, MAN! THEN I'M COMING WITH YOU.
FINE. JUST STAY QUIET, OKAY?

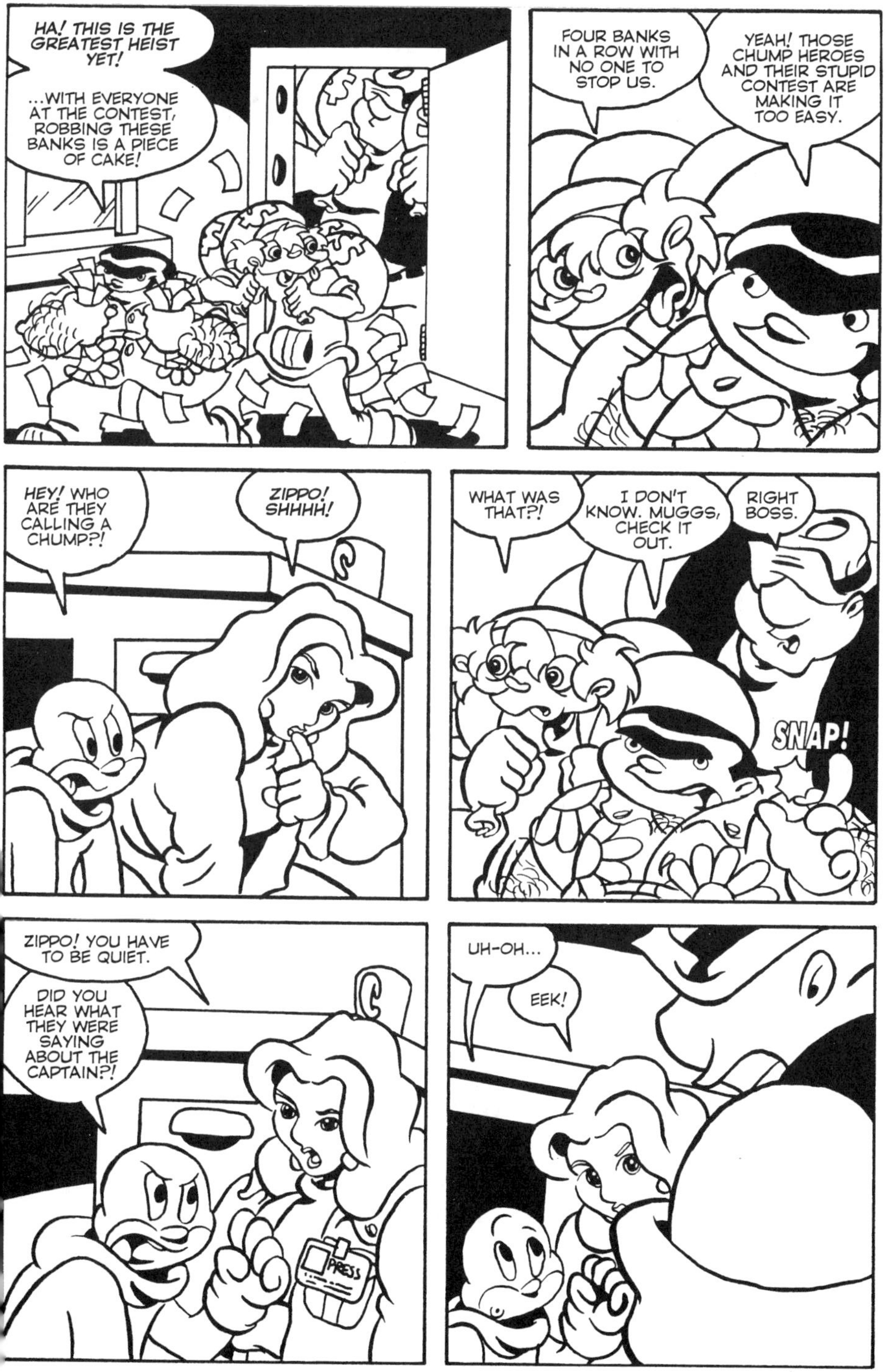
HA! THIS IS THE GREATEST HEIST YET!
...WITH EVERYONE AT THE CONTEST, ROBBING THESE BANKS IS A PIECE OF CAKE!
FOUR BANKS IN A ROW WITH NO ONE TO STOP US.
YEAH! THOSE CHUMP HEROES AND THEIR STUPID CONTEST ARE MAKING IT TOO EASY.
HEY! WHO ARE THEY CALLING A CHUMP?!
ZIPPO! SHHHH!
WHAT WAS THAT?!
I DON'T KNOW. MUGGS, CHECK IT OUT.
RIGHT BOSS.
SNAP!
ZIPPO! YOU HAVE TO BE QUIET.
DID YOU HEAR WHAT THEY WERE SAYING ABOUT THE CAPTAIN?!
PRESS
UH-OH...
EEK!

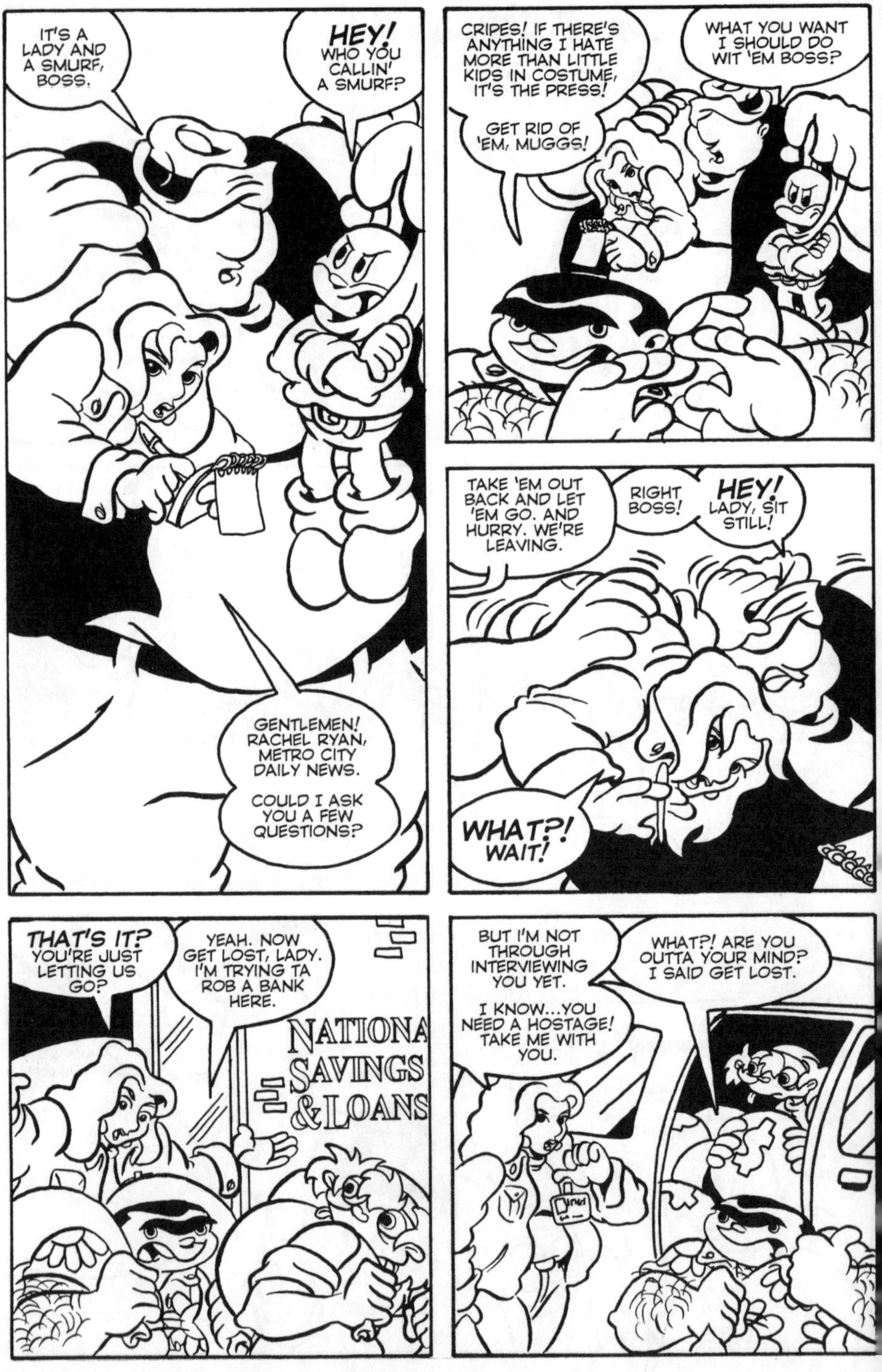
IT'S A LADY AND A SMURF, BOSS.
HEY! WHO YOU CALLIN' A SMURF?
GENTLEMEN! RACHEL RYAN, METRO CITY DAILY NEWS.
COULD I ASK YOU A FEW QUESTIONS?
CRIPES! IF THERE'S ANYTHING I HATE MORE THAN LITTLE KIDS IN COSTUME, IT'S THE PRESS!
GET RID OF 'EM, MUGGS!
WHAT YOU WANT I SHOULD DO WIT 'EM BOSS?
TAKE 'EM OUT BACK AND LET 'EM GO. AND HURRY. WE'RE LEAVING.
RIGHT BOSS!
HEY! LADY, SIT STILL!
WHAT?! WAIT!
THAT'S IT? YOU'RE JUST LETTING US GO?
YEAH. NOW GET LOST, LADY. I'M TRYING TA ROB A BANK HERE.
NATIONA SAVINGS & LOANS
BUT I'M NOT THROUGH INTERVIEWING YOU YET.
I KNOW... YOU NEED A HOSTAGE! TAKE ME WITH YOU.
WHAT?! ARE YOU OUTTA YOUR MIND? I SAID GET LOST.

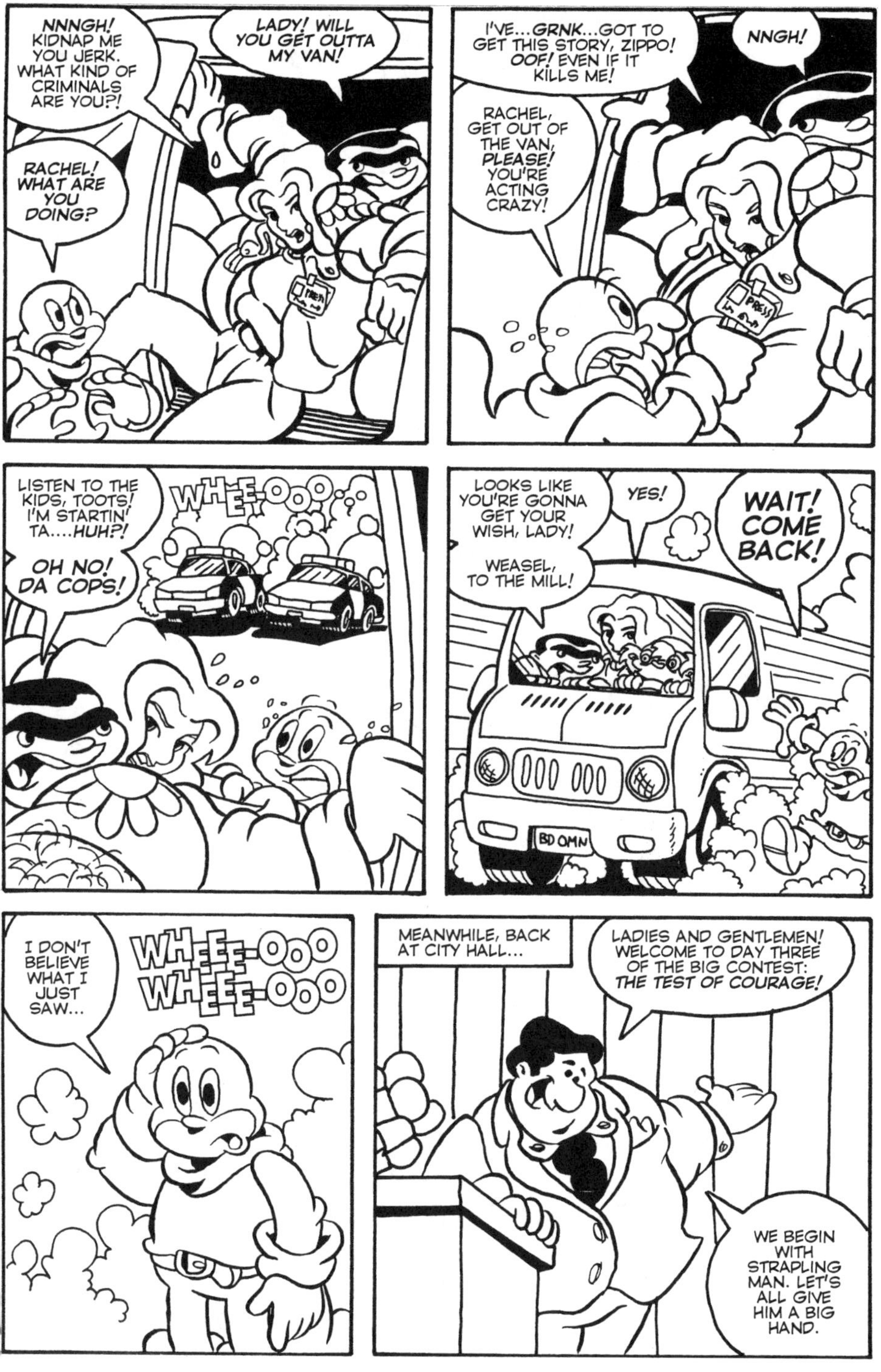
NNNGH! KIDNAP ME YOU JERK. WHAT KIND OF CRIMINALS ARE YOU?!
LADY! WILL YOU GET OUTTA MY VAN!
RACHEL! WHAT ARE YOU DOING?
PRESS
I'VE...GRNK...GOT TO GET THIS STORY, ZIPPO! OOF! EVEN IF IT KILLS ME!
NNGH!
RACHEL, GET OUT OF THE VAN, PLEASE! YOU'RE ACTING CRAZY!
PRESS
LISTEN TO THE KIDS, TOOTS! I'M STARTIN' TA....HUH?!
WHEE-OOO
OH NO! DA COPS!
LOOKS LIKE YOU'RE GONNA GET YOUR WISH, LADY!
WEASEL, TO THE MILL!
YES!
WAIT! COME BACK!
BD OMN
I DON'T BELIEVE WHAT I JUST SAW...
WHEEE-OOO
WHEEE-OOO
MEANWHILE, BACK AT CITY HALL...
LADIES AND GENTLEMEN! WELCOME TO DAY THREE OF THE BIG CONTEST: THE TEST OF COURAGE!
WE BEGIN WITH STRAPLING MAN. LET'S ALL GIVE HIM A BIG HAND.

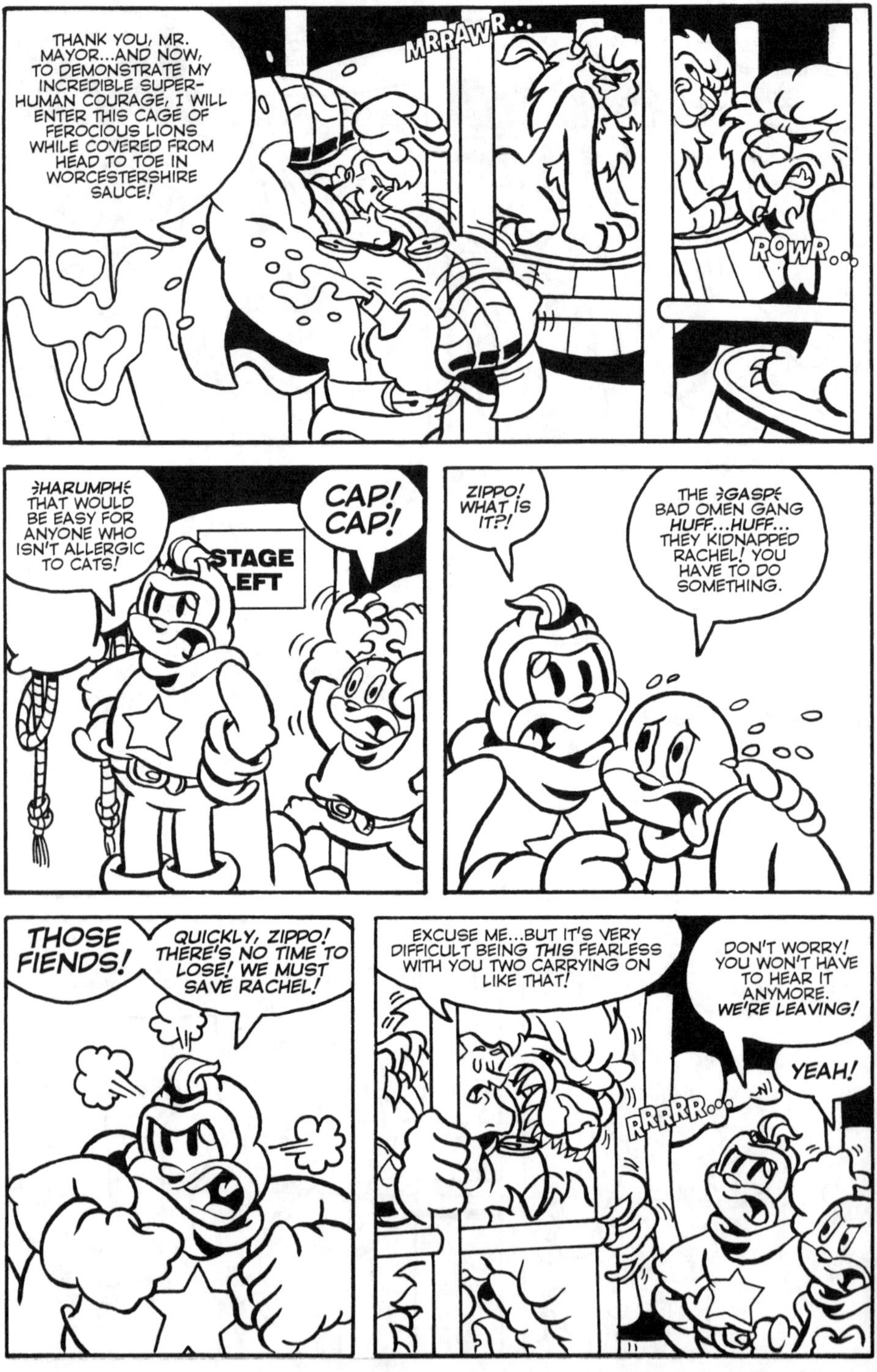
THANK YOU, MR. MAYOR...AND NOW, TO DEMONSTRATE MY INCREDIBLE SUPER-HUMAN COURAGE, I WILL ENTER THIS CAGE OF FEROCIOUS LIONS WHILE COVERED FROM HEAD TO TOE IN WORCESTERSHIRE SAUCE!
MRRAWR...
ROWR...
HARUMPH THAT WOULD BE EASY FOR ANYONE WHO ISN'T ALLERGIC TO CATS!
STAGE LEFT
CAP! CAP!
ZIPPO! WHAT IS IT?!
THE GASP BAD OMEN GANG HUFF...HUFF... THEY KIDNAPPED RACHEL! YOU HAVE TO DO SOMETHING.
THOSE FIENDS!
QUICKLY, ZIPPO! THERE'S NO TIME TO LOSE! WE MUST SAVE RACHEL!
EXCUSE ME...BUT IT'S VERY DIFFICULT BEING THIS FEARLESS WITH YOU TWO CARRYING ON LIKE THAT!
DON'T WORRY! YOU WON'T HAVE TO HEAR IT ANYMORE. WE'RE LEAVING!
YEAH!
RRRRR...

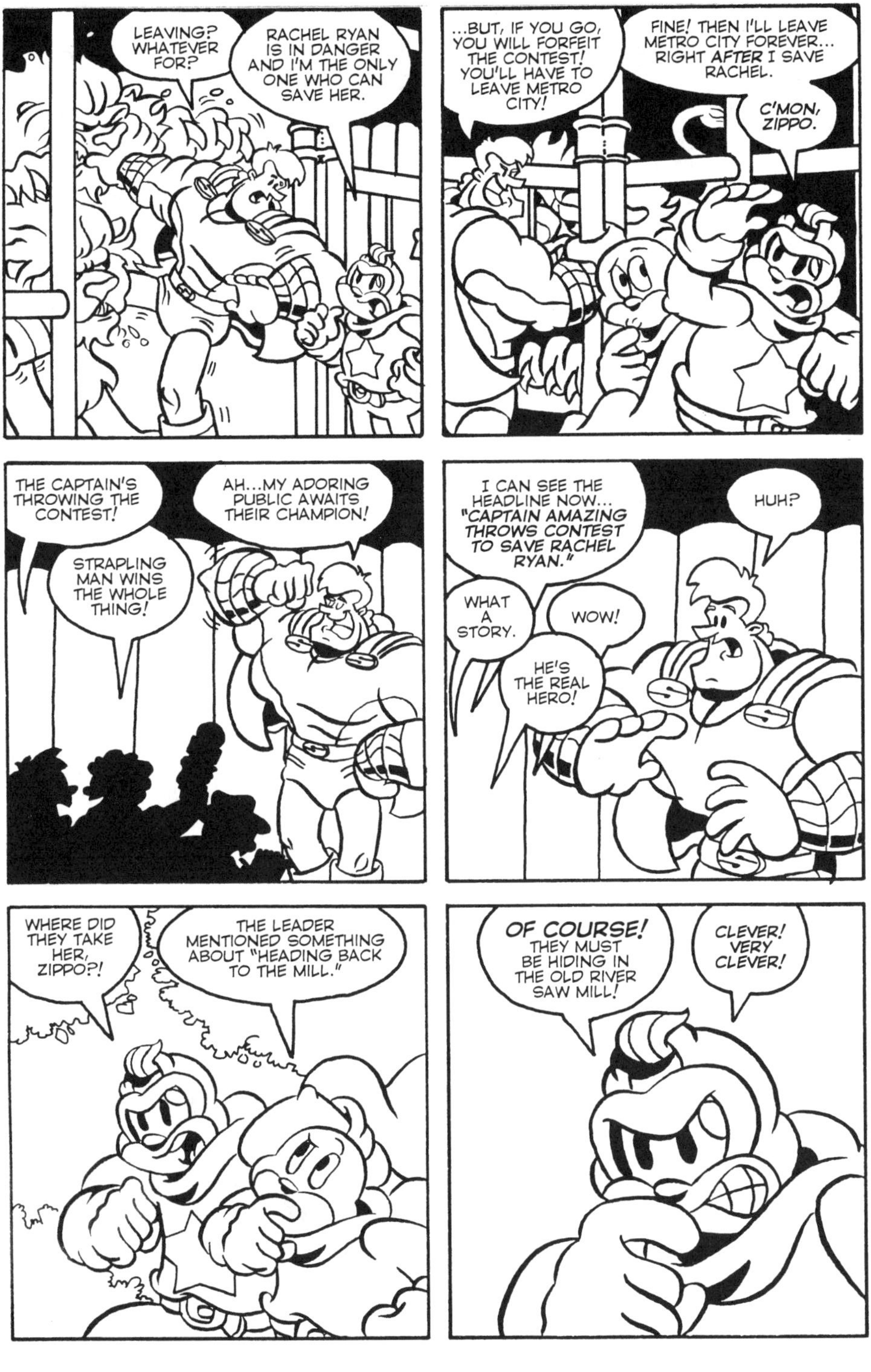
LEAVING? WHATEVER FOR?
RACHEL RYAN IS IN DANGER AND I'M THE ONLY ONE WHO CAN SAVE HER.
...BUT, IF YOU GO, YOU WILL FORFEIT THE CONTEST! YOU'LL HAVE TO LEAVE METRO CITY!
FINE! THEN I'LL LEAVE METRO CITY FOREVER... RIGHT AFTER I SAVE RACHEL.
C'MON, ZIPPO.
THE CAPTAIN'S THROWING THE CONTEST!
STRAPLING MAN WINS THE WHOLE THING!
AH...MY ADORING PUBLIC AWAITS THEIR CHAMPION!
I CAN SEE THE HEADLINE NOW... "CAPTAIN AMAZING THROWS CONTEST TO SAVE RACHEL RYAN."
HUH?
WHAT A STORY.
WOW!
HE'S THE REAL HERO!
WHERE DID THEY TAKE HER, ZIPPO?!
THE LEADER MENTIONED SOMETHING ABOUT "HEADING BACK TO THE MILL."
OF COURSE! THEY MUST BE HIDING IN THE OLD RIVER SAW MILL!
CLEVER! VERY CLEVER!

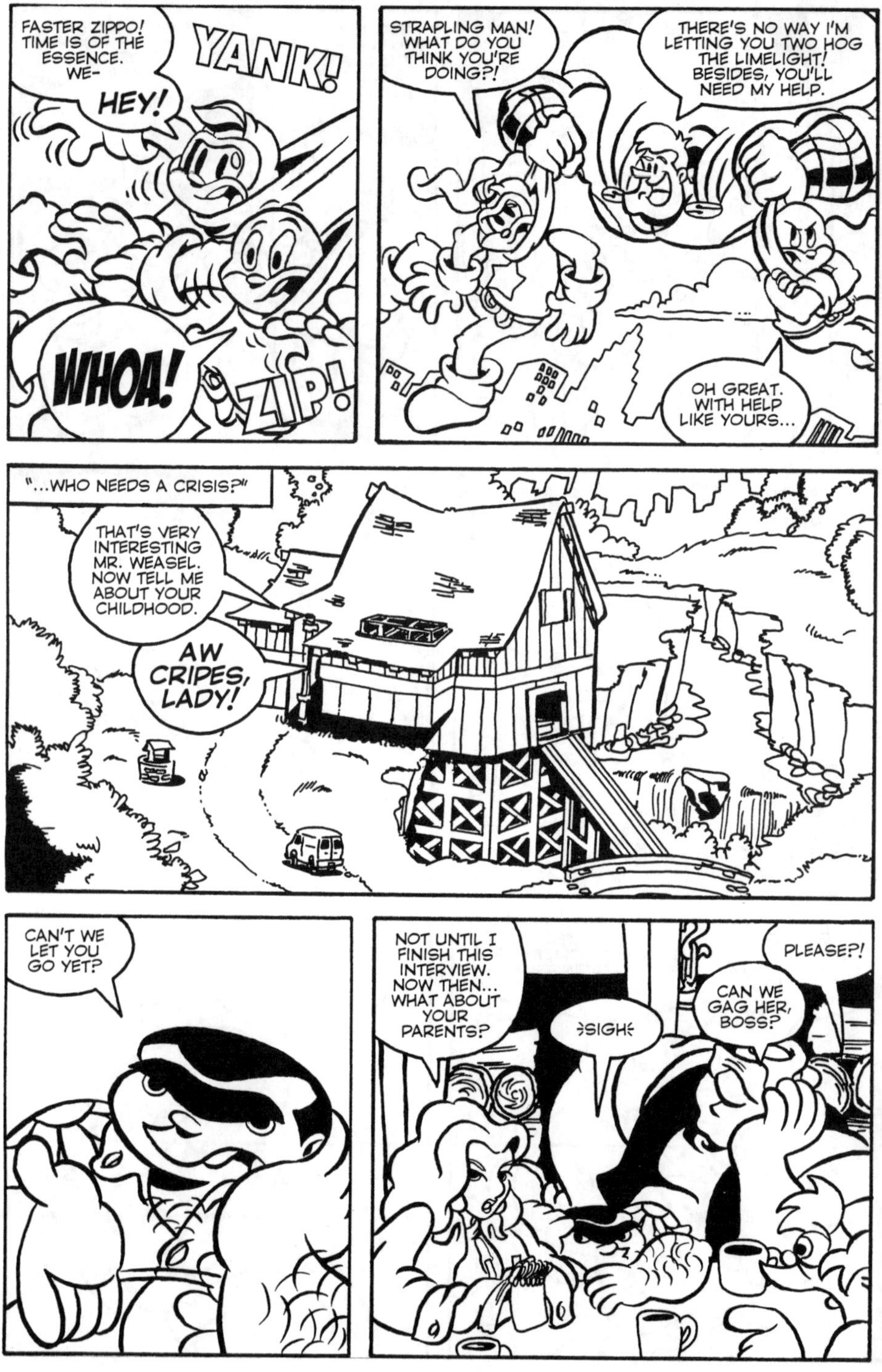
FASTER ZIPPO! TIME IS OF THE ESSENCE. WE-
YANK!
HEY!
WHOA!
ZIP!
STRAPLING MAN! WHAT DO YOU THINK YOU'RE DOING?!
THERE'S NO WAY I'M LETTING YOU TWO HOG THE LIMELIGHT! BESIDES, YOU'LL NEED MY HELP.
OH GREAT. WITH HELP LIKE YOURS...
"...WHO NEEDS A CRISIS?"
THAT'S VERY INTERESTING MR. WEASEL. NOW TELL ME ABOUT YOUR CHILDHOOD.
AW CRIPES, LADY!
CAN'T WE LET YOU GO YET?
NOT UNTIL I FINISH THIS INTERVIEW. NOW THEN... WHAT ABOUT YOUR PARENTS?
SIGH
PLEASE?!
CAN WE GAG HER, BOSS?

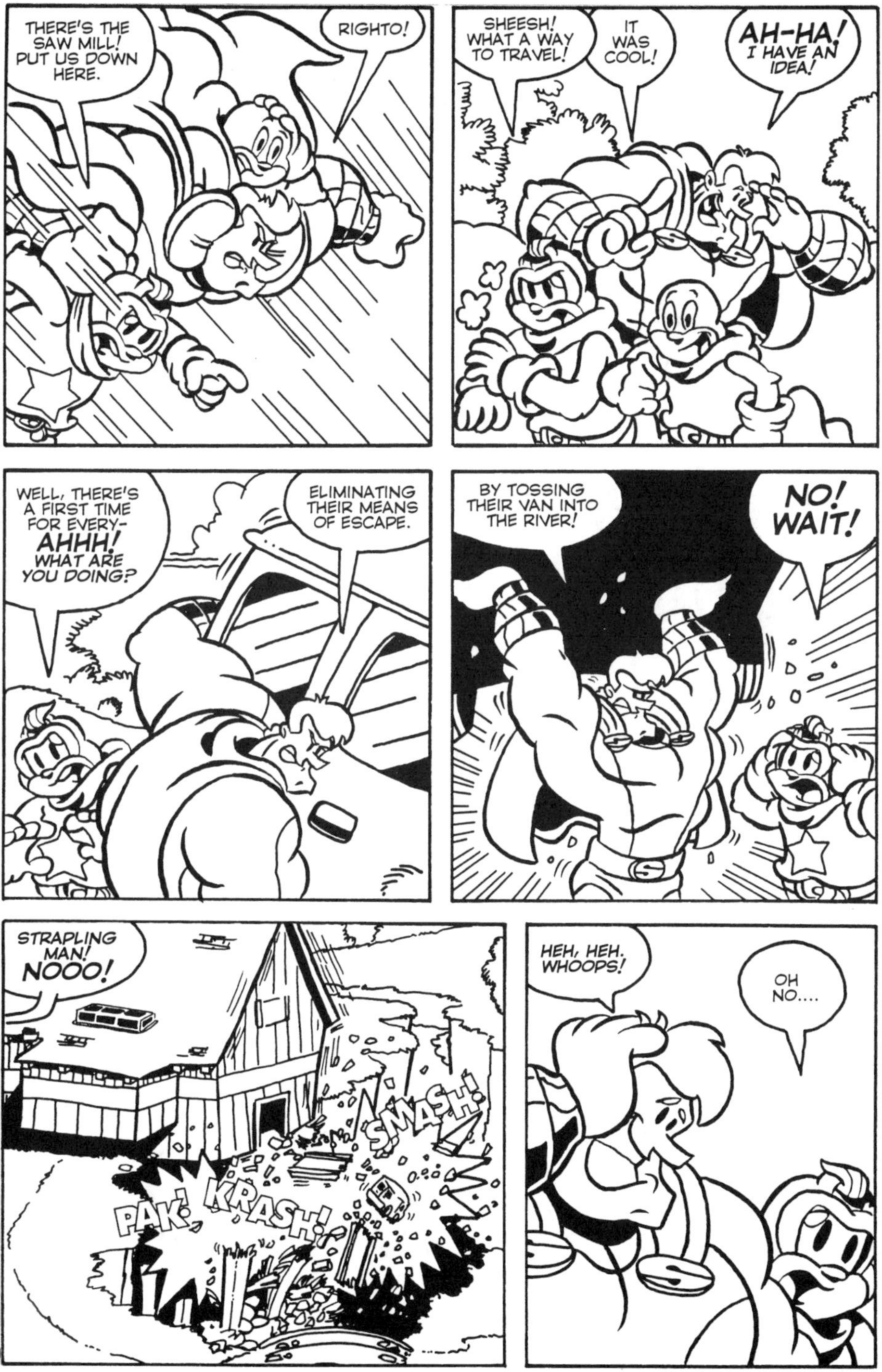
THERE'S THE SAW MILL! PUT US DOWN HERE.
RIGHTO!
SHEESH! WHAT A WAY TO TRAVEL!
IT WAS COOL!
AH-HA! I HAVE AN IDEA!
WELL, THERE'S A FIRST TIME FOR EVERY- AHHH! WHAT ARE YOU DOING?
ELIMINATING THEIR MEANS OF ESCAPE.
BY TOSSING THEIR VAN INTO THE RIVER!
NO! WAIT!
STRAPLING MAN! NOOO!
SMASH!
PAK! KRASH!
HEH, HEH. WHOOPS!
OH NO....

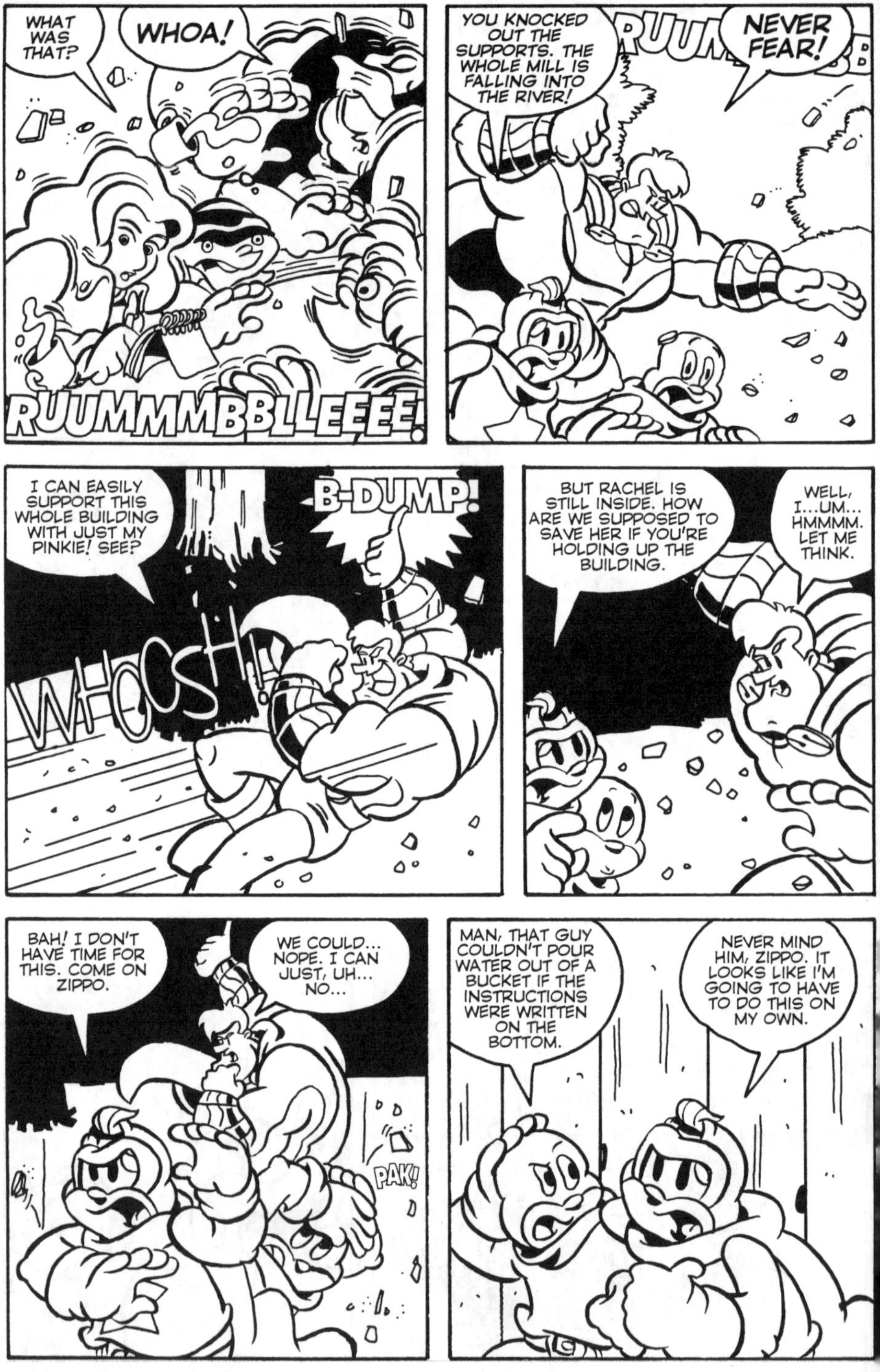
WHAT WAS THAT?
WHOA!
RUUMMMMBBLLEEEE!
YOU KNOCKED OUT THE SUPPORTS. THE WHOLE MILL IS FALLING INTO THE RIVER!
RUUM
NEVER FEAR!
I CAN EASILY SUPPORT THIS WHOLE BUILDING WITH JUST MY PINKIE! SEE?
B-DUMP!
WHOOSH!
BUT RACHEL IS STILL INSIDE. HOW ARE WE SUPPOSED TO SAVE HER IF YOU'RE HOLDING UP THE BUILDING.
WELL, I...UM... HMMMM. LET ME THINK.
BAH! I DON'T HAVE TIME FOR THIS. COME ON ZIPPO.
WE COULD... NOPE. I CAN JUST, UH... NO...
PAK!
MAN, THAT GUY COULDN'T POUR WATER OUT OF A BUCKET IF THE INSTRUCTIONS WERE WRITTEN ON THE BOTTOM.
NEVER MIND HIM, ZIPPO. IT LOOKS LIKE I'M GOING TO HAVE TO DO THIS ON MY OWN.

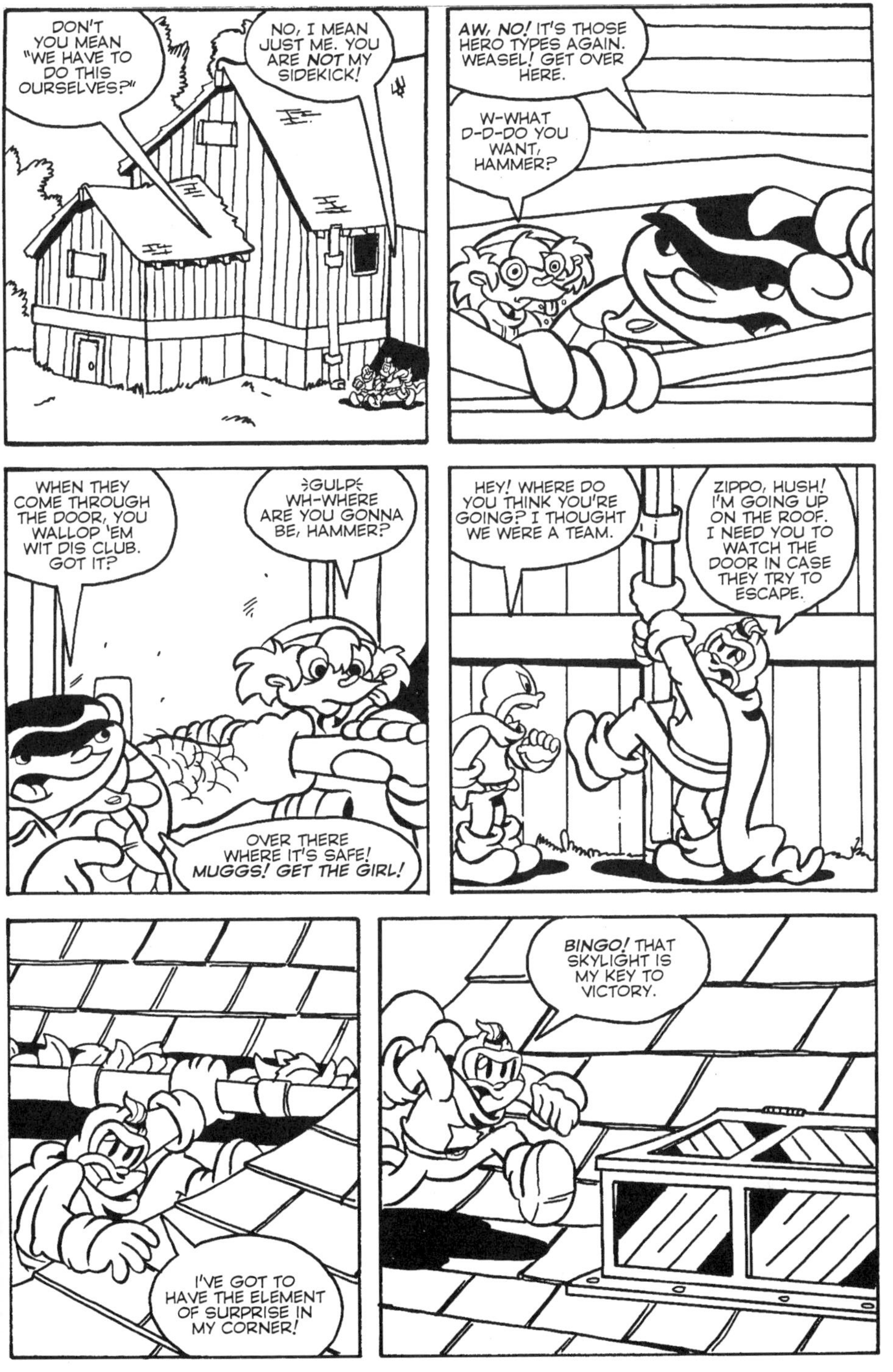
DON'T YOU MEAN "WE HAVE TO DO THIS OURSELVES?"
NO, I MEAN JUST ME. YOU ARE *NOT* MY SIDEKICK!
AW, NO! IT'S THOSE HERO TYPES AGAIN. WEASEL! GET OVER HERE.
W-WHAT D-D-DO YOU WANT, HAMMER?
WHEN THEY COME THROUGH THE DOOR, YOU WALLOP 'EM WIT DIS CLUB. GOT IT?
GULP WH-WHERE ARE YOU GONNA BE, HAMMER?
OVER THERE WHERE IT'S SAFE! *MUGGS! GET THE GIRL!*
HEY! WHERE DO YOU THINK YOU'RE GOING? I THOUGHT WE WERE A TEAM.
ZIPPO, HUSH! I'M GOING UP ON THE ROOF. I NEED YOU TO WATCH THE DOOR IN CASE THEY TRY TO ESCAPE.
I'VE GOT TO HAVE THE ELEMENT OF SURPRISE IN MY CORNER!
BINGO! THAT SKYLIGHT IS MY KEY TO VICTORY.

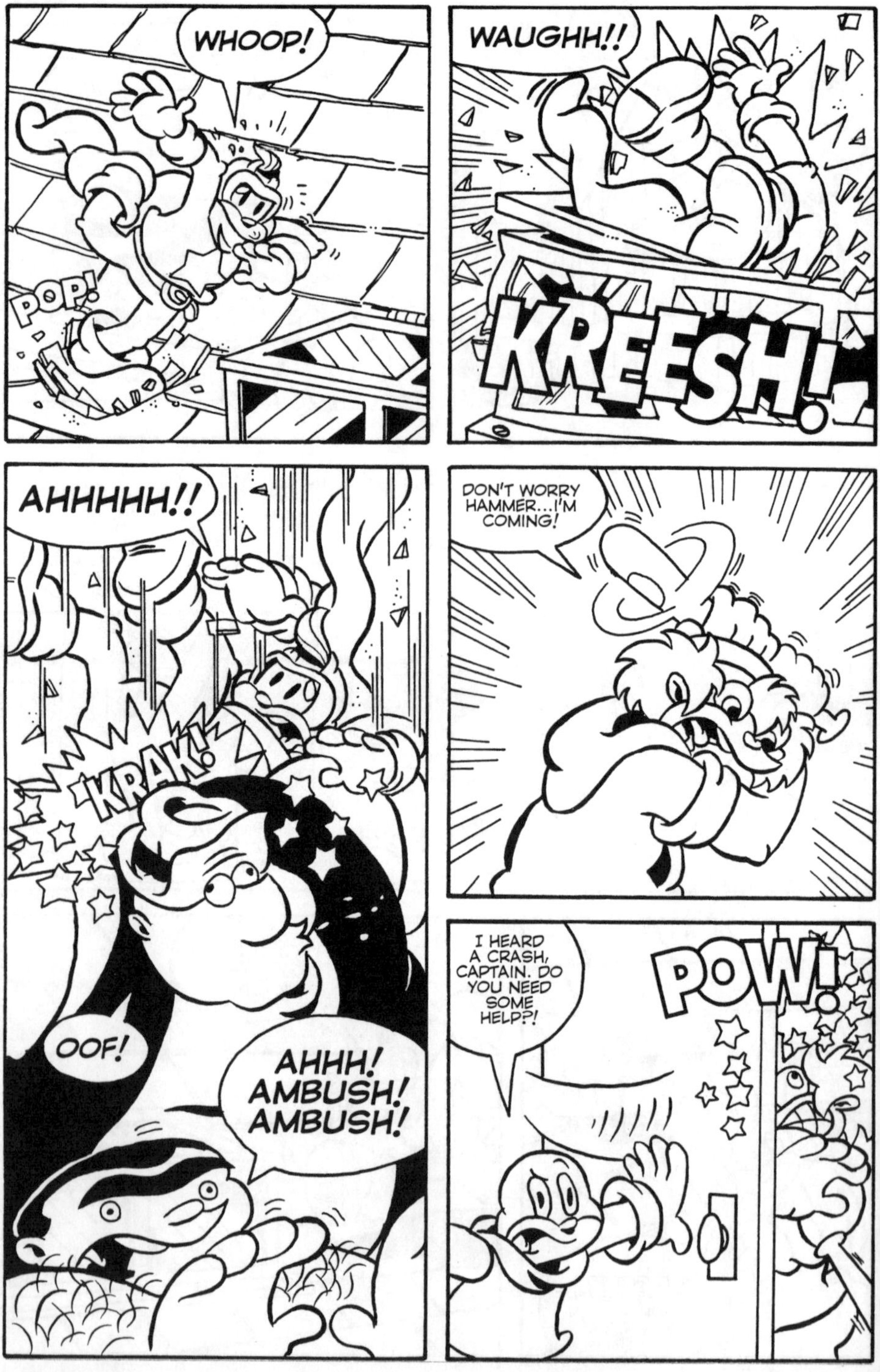
WHOOP!
POP!
WAUGHH!!
KREESH!
AHHHHH!!
KRAK!
OOF!
AHHH! AMBUSH! AMBUSH!
DON'T WORRY HAMMER...I'M COMING!
I HEARD A CRASH, CAPTAIN. DO YOU NEED SOME HELP?!
POW!

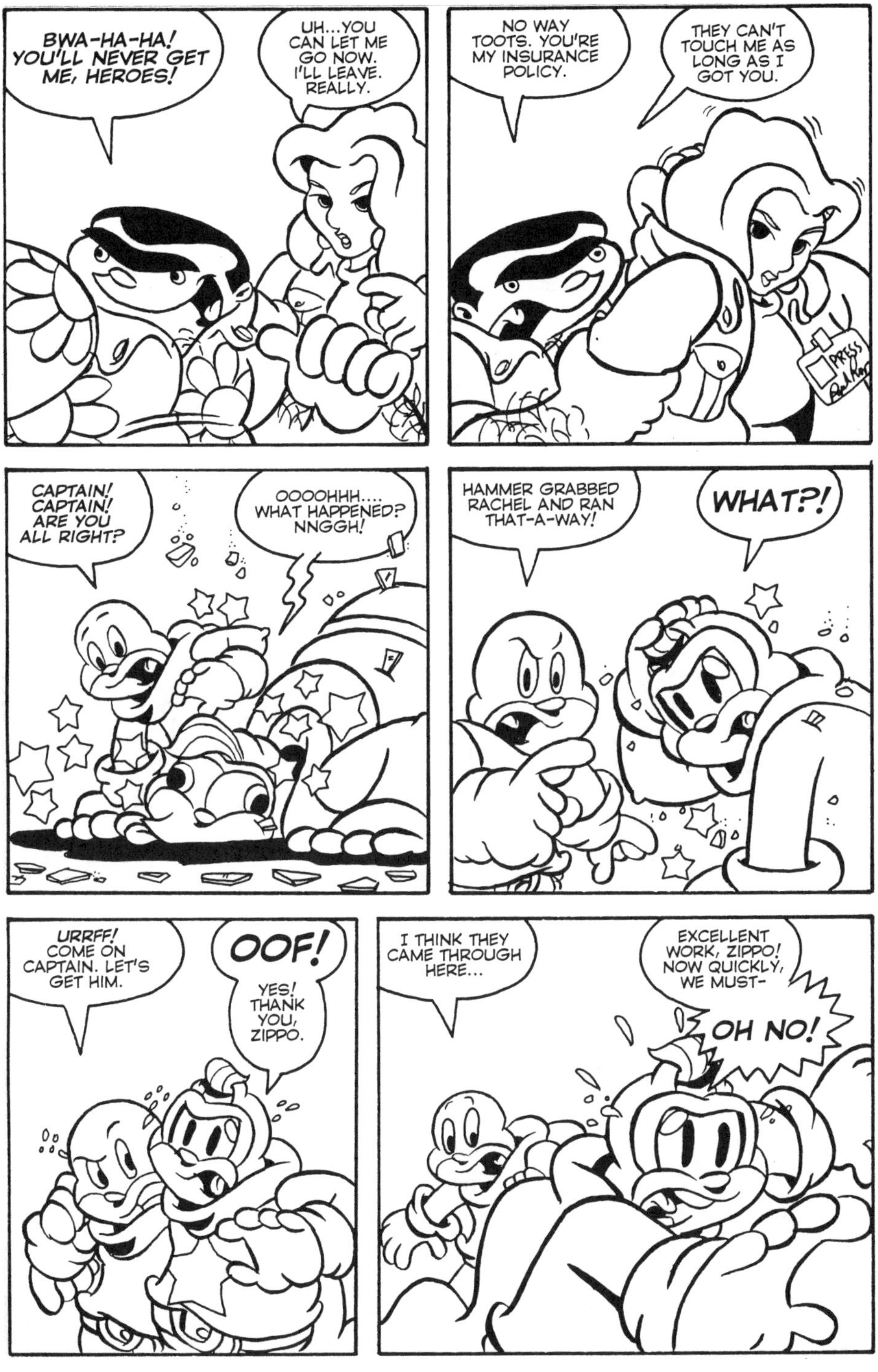
BWA-HA-HA! YOU'LL NEVER GET ME, HEROES!
UH...YOU CAN LET ME GO NOW. I'LL LEAVE. REALLY.
NO WAY TOOTS. YOU'RE MY INSURANCE POLICY.
THEY CAN'T TOUCH ME AS LONG AS I GOT YOU.
PRESS
CAPTAIN! CAPTAIN! ARE YOU ALL RIGHT?
OOOOHHH.... WHAT HAPPENED? NNGGH!
HAMMER GRABBED RACHEL AND RAN THAT-A-WAY!
WHAT?!
URRFF! COME ON CAPTAIN. LET'S GET HIM.
OOF!
YES! THANK YOU, ZIPPO.
I THINK THEY CAME THROUGH HERE...
EXCELLENT WORK, ZIPPO! NOW QUICKLY, WE MUST-
OH NO!

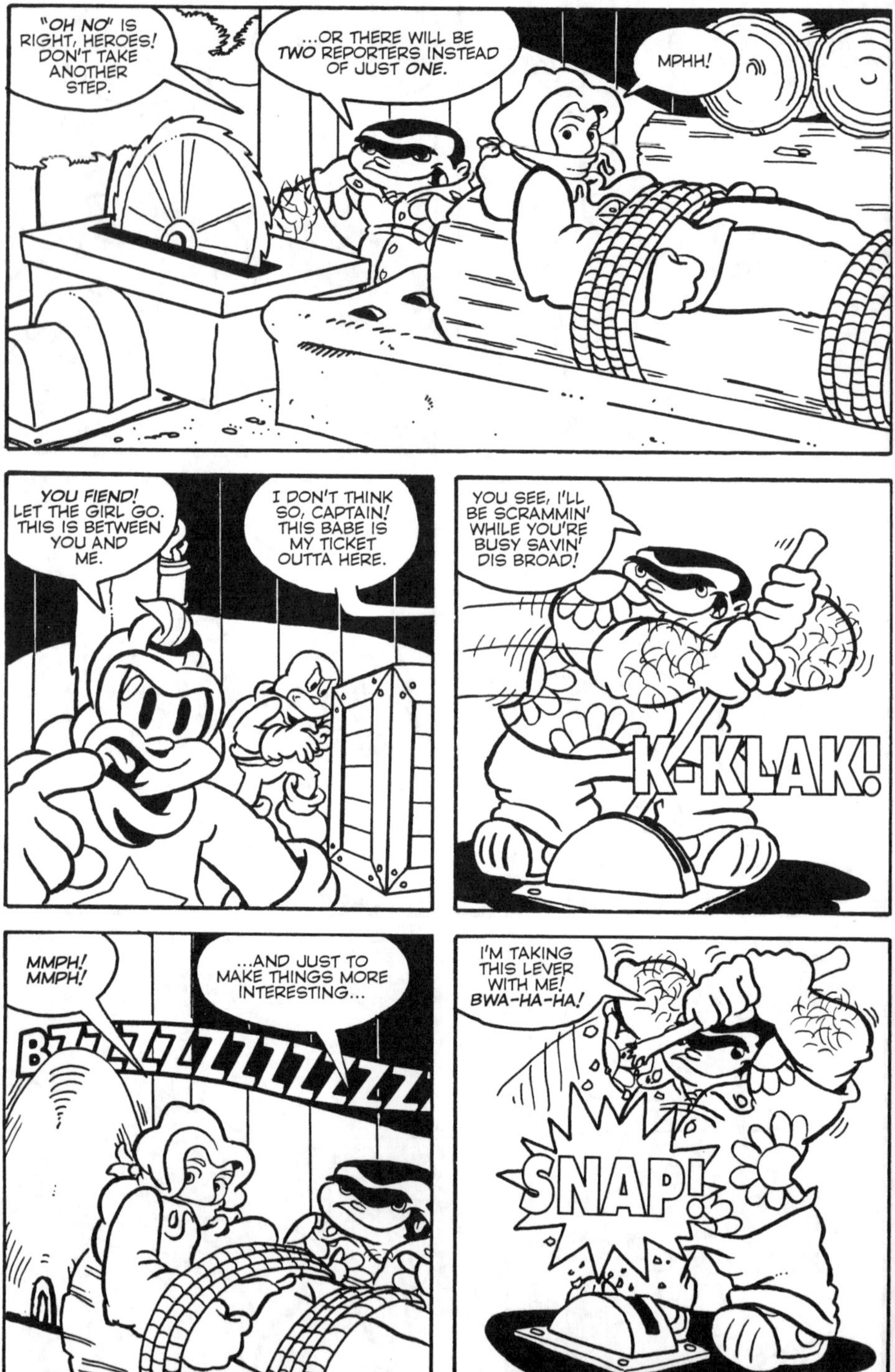
"OH NO" IS RIGHT, HEROES! DON'T TAKE ANOTHER STEP.
...OR THERE WILL BE TWO REPORTERS INSTEAD OF JUST ONE.
MPHH!
YOU FIEND! LET THE GIRL GO. THIS IS BETWEEN YOU AND ME.
I DON'T THINK SO, CAPTAIN! THIS BABE IS MY TICKET OUTTA HERE.
YOU SEE, I'LL BE SCRAMMIN' WHILE YOU'RE BUSY SAVIN' DIS BROAD!
K-KLAK!
MMPH! MMPH!
...AND JUST TO MAKE THINGS MORE INTERESTING...
I'M TAKING THIS LEVER WITH ME! BWA-HA-HA!
SNAP!

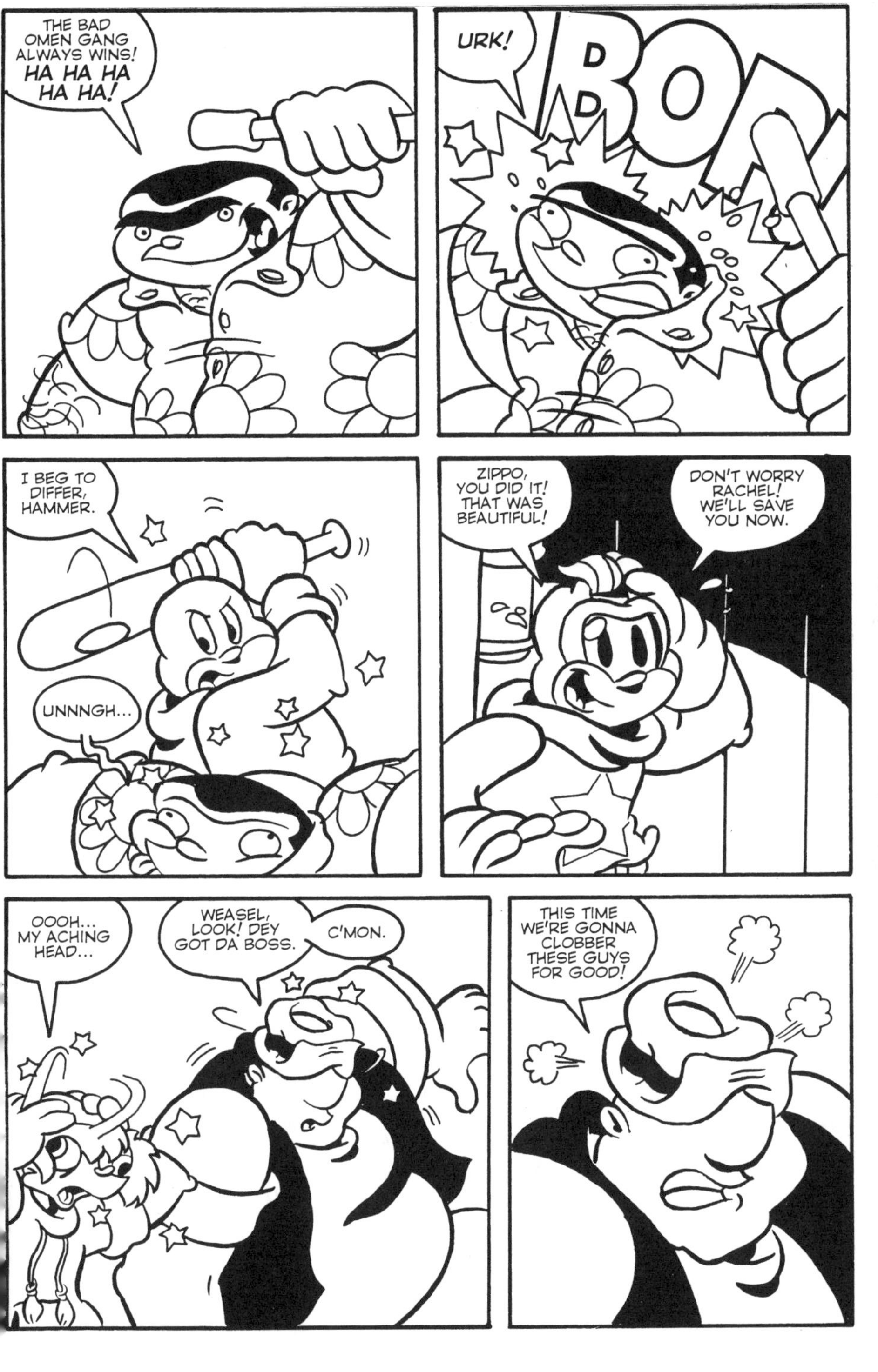
THE BAD OMEN GANG ALWAYS WINS! HA HA HA HA HA!
URK!
BOD
I BEG TO DIFFER, HAMMER.
UNNNGH...
ZIPPO, YOU DID IT! THAT WAS BEAUTIFUL!
DON'T WORRY RACHEL! WE'LL SAVE YOU NOW.
OOOH... MY ACHING HEAD...
WEASEL, LOOK! DEY GOT DA BOSS.
C'MON.
THIS TIME WE'RE GONNA CLOBBER THESE GUYS FOR GOOD!

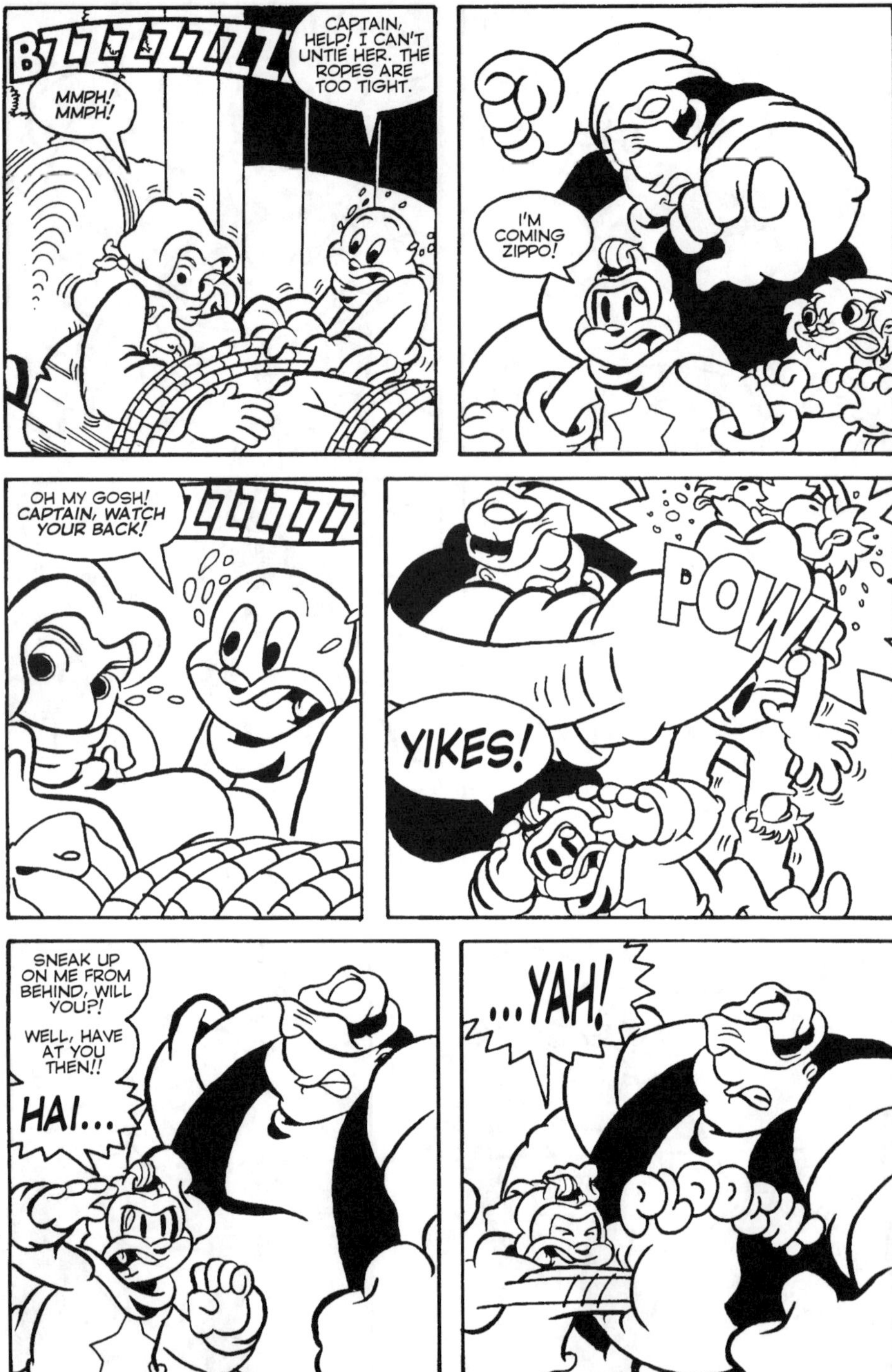
BZZZZZZZZZ
MMPH! MMPH!
CAPTAIN, HELP! I CAN'T UNTIE HER. THE ROPES ARE TOO TIGHT.
I'M COMING ZIPPO!
OH MY GOSH! CAPTAIN, WATCH YOUR BACK!
ZZZZZZZ
POW!
YIKES!
SNEAK UP ON ME FROM BEHIND, WILL YOU?!
WELL, HAVE AT YOU THEN!!
HAI...
...YAH!
PLOOF!

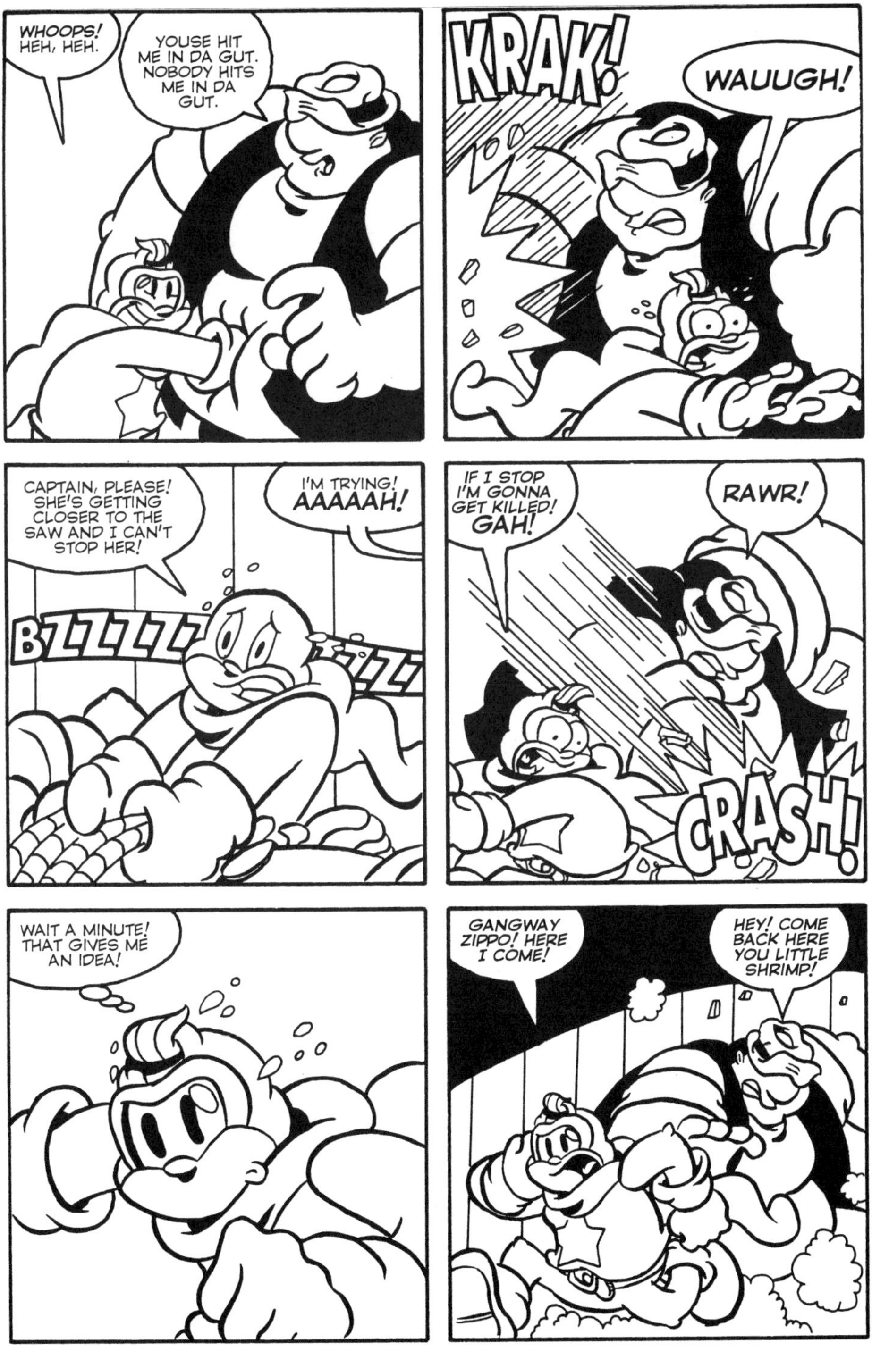
WHOOPS! HEH, HEH.
YOUSE HIT ME IN DA GUT. NOBODY HITS ME IN DA GUT.
KRAK!
WAUUGH!
CAPTAIN, PLEASE! SHE'S GETTING CLOSER TO THE SAW AND I CAN'T STOP HER!
I'M TRYING! AAAAAH!
BZZZZZZZZZ
IF I STOP I'M GONNA GET KILLED! GAH!
RAWR!
CRASH!
WAIT A MINUTE! THAT GIVES ME AN IDEA!
GANGWAY ZIPPO! HERE I COME!
HEY! COME BACK HERE YOU LITTLE SHRIMP!

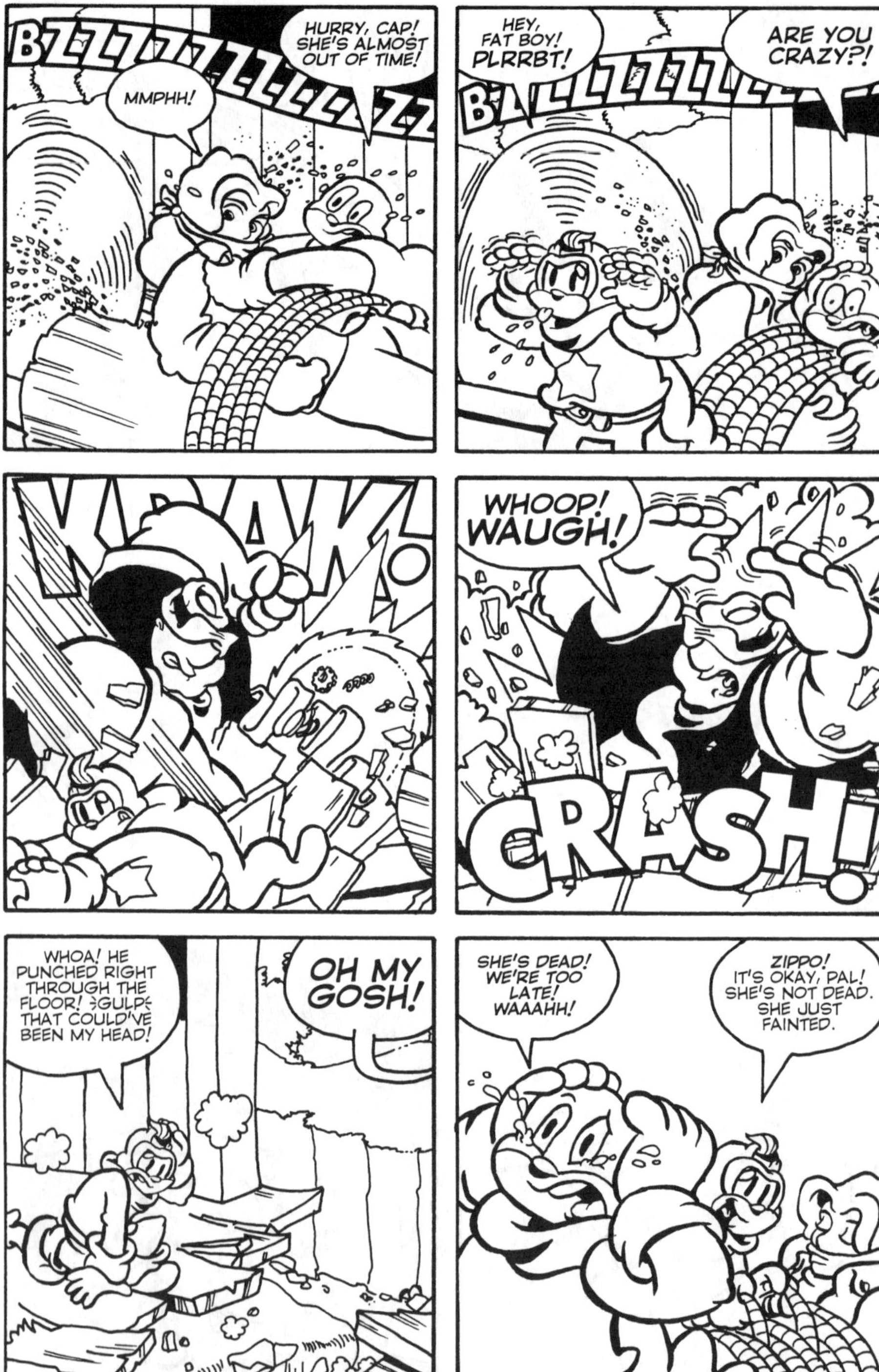
HURRY, CAP! SHE'S ALMOST OUT OF TIME!
MMPHH!
HEY, FAT BOY! PLRRBT!
ARE YOU CRAZY?!
WHOOP! WAUGH!
CRASH!
WHOA! HE PUNCHED RIGHT THROUGH THE FLOOR! GULP THAT COULD'VE BEEN MY HEAD!
OH MY GOSH!
SHE'S DEAD! WE'RE TOO LATE! WAAAHH!
ZIPPO! IT'S OKAY, PAL! SHE'S NOT DEAD. SHE JUST FAINTED.

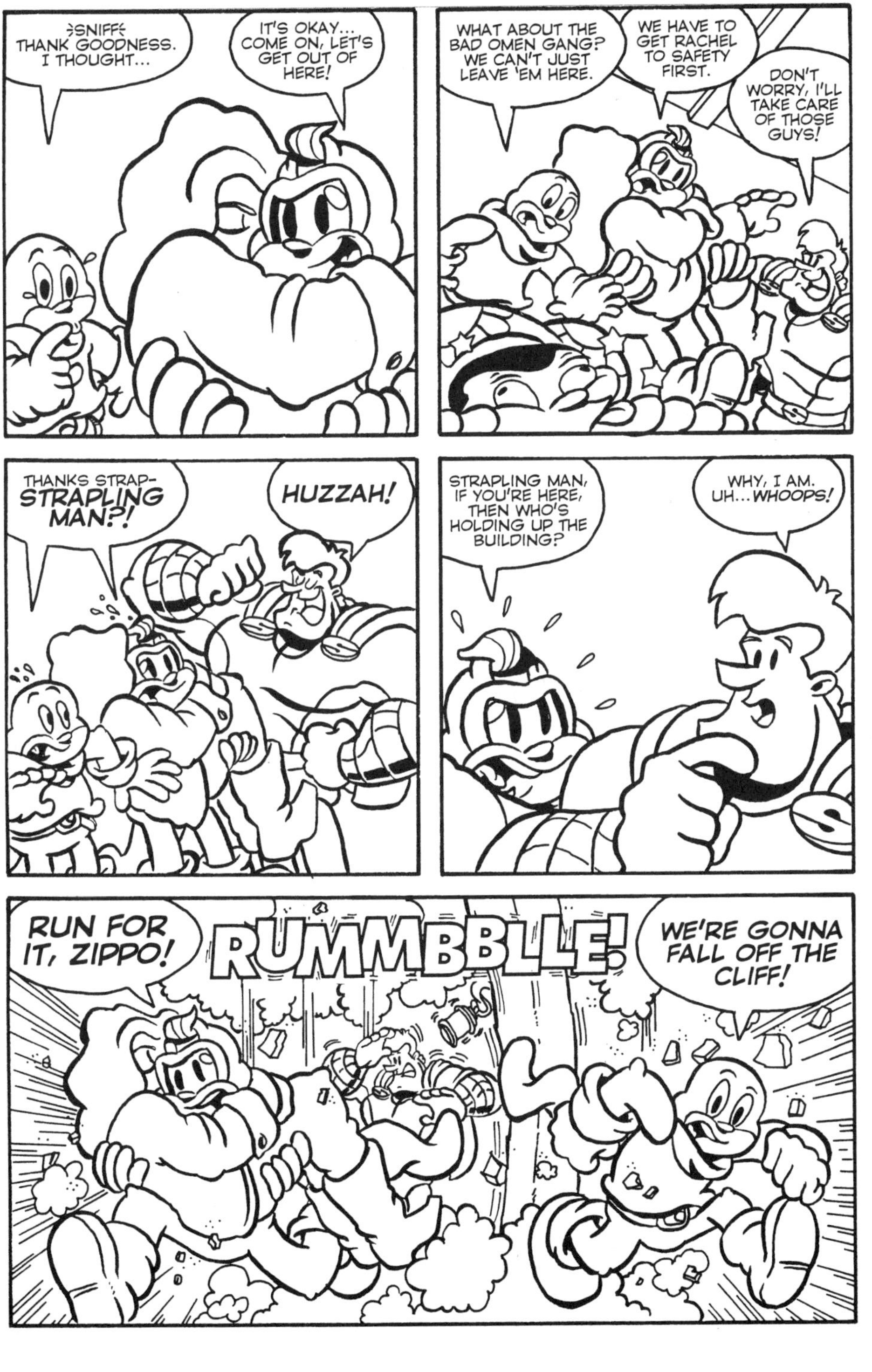

≈SNIFF≈ THANK GOODNESS. I THOUGHT...
IT'S OKAY... COME ON, LET'S GET OUT OF HERE!
WHAT ABOUT THE BAD OMEN GANG? WE CAN'T JUST LEAVE 'EM HERE.
WE HAVE TO GET RACHEL TO SAFETY FIRST.
DON'T WORRY, I'LL TAKE CARE OF THOSE GUYS!
THANKS STRAP- STRAPLING MAN?!
HUZZAH!
STRAPLING MAN, IF YOU'RE HERE, THEN WHO'S HOLDING UP THE BUILDING?
WHY, I AM. UH...WHOOPS!
RUN FOR IT, ZIPPO!
RUMMBBLLE!
WE'RE GONNA FALL OFF THE CLIFF!

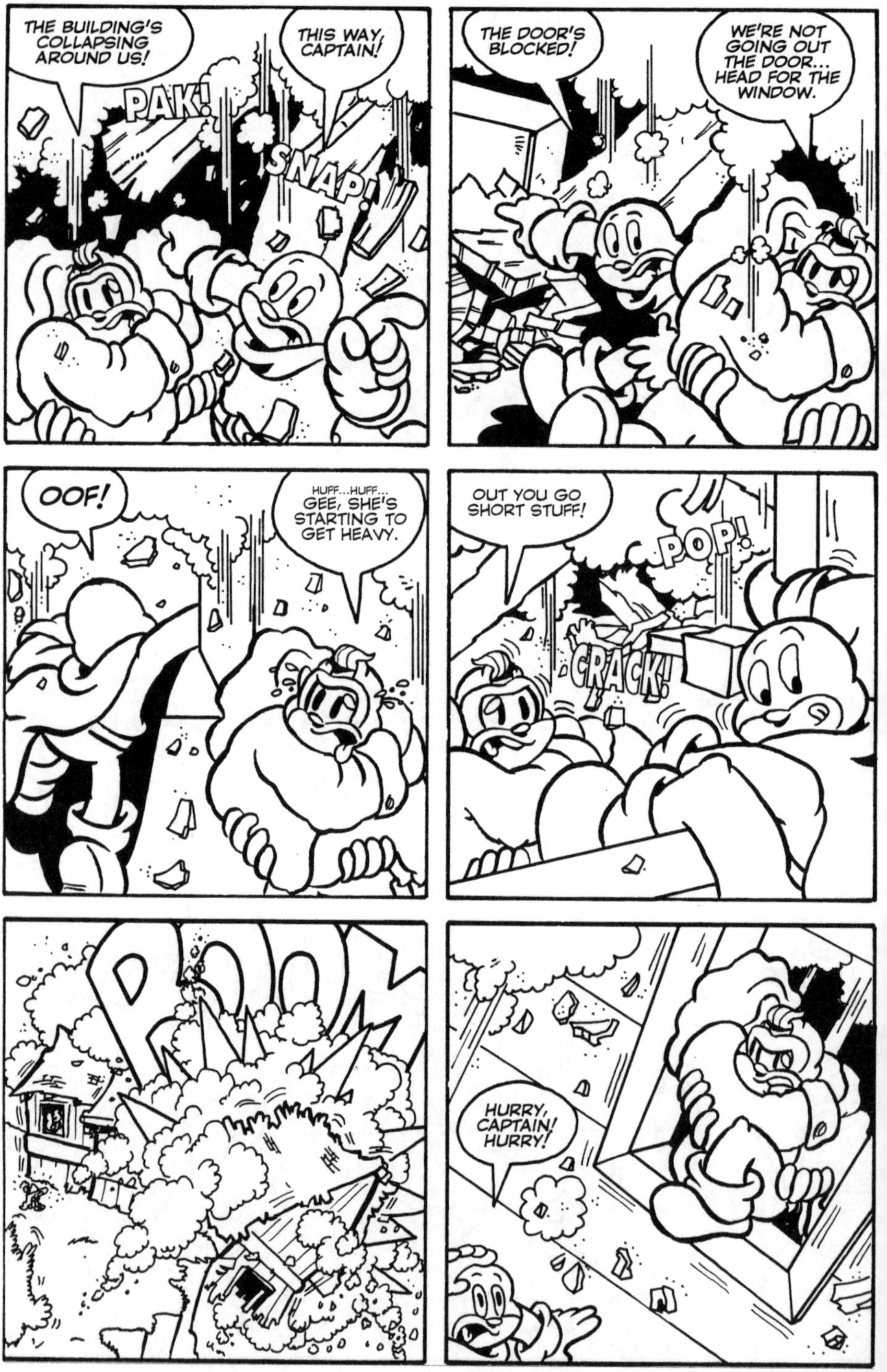
THE BUILDING'S COLLAPSING AROUND US!
THIS WAY, CAPTAIN!
PAK!
SNAP!
THE DOOR'S BLOCKED!
WE'RE NOT GOING OUT THE DOOR... HEAD FOR THE WINDOW.
OOF!
HUFF...HUFF... GEE, SHE'S STARTING TO GET HEAVY.
OUT YOU GO SHORT STUFF!
POP!
CRACK!
HURRY, CAPTAIN! HURRY!

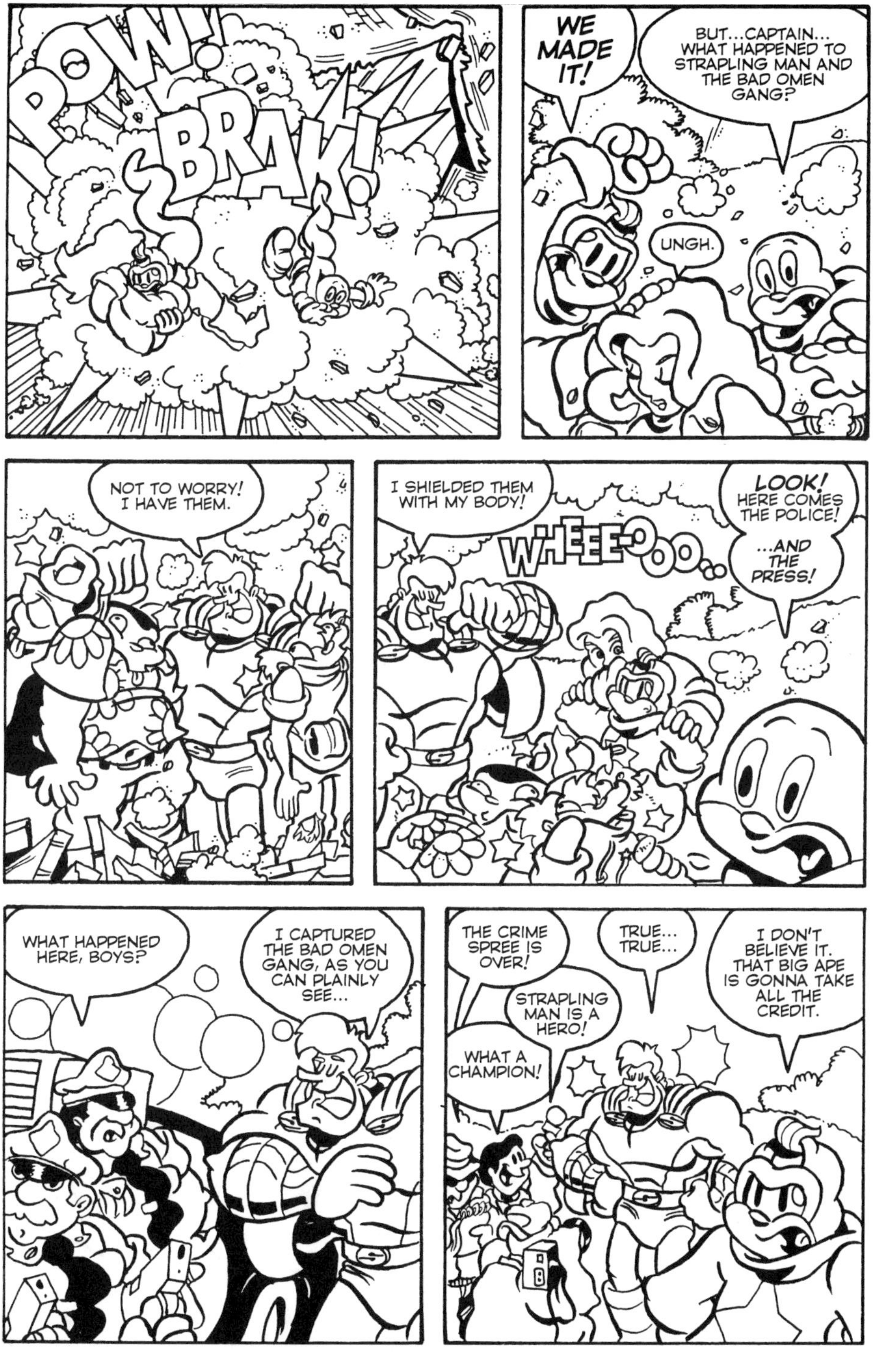
POW!
BRAK!
WE MADE IT!
BUT...CAPTAIN... WHAT HAPPENED TO STRAPLING MAN AND THE BAD OMEN GANG?
UNGH.
NOT TO WORRY! I HAVE THEM.
I SHIELDED THEM WITH MY BODY!
WHEEE-OOO...
LOOK! HERE COMES THE POLICE!
...AND THE PRESS!
WHAT HAPPENED HERE, BOYS?
I CAPTURED THE BAD OMEN GANG, AS YOU CAN PLAINLY SEE...
THE CRIME SPREE IS OVER!
TRUE... TRUE...
I DON'T BELIEVE IT. THAT BIG APE IS GONNA TAKE ALL THE CREDIT.
STRAPLING MAN IS A HERO!
WHAT A CHAMPION!

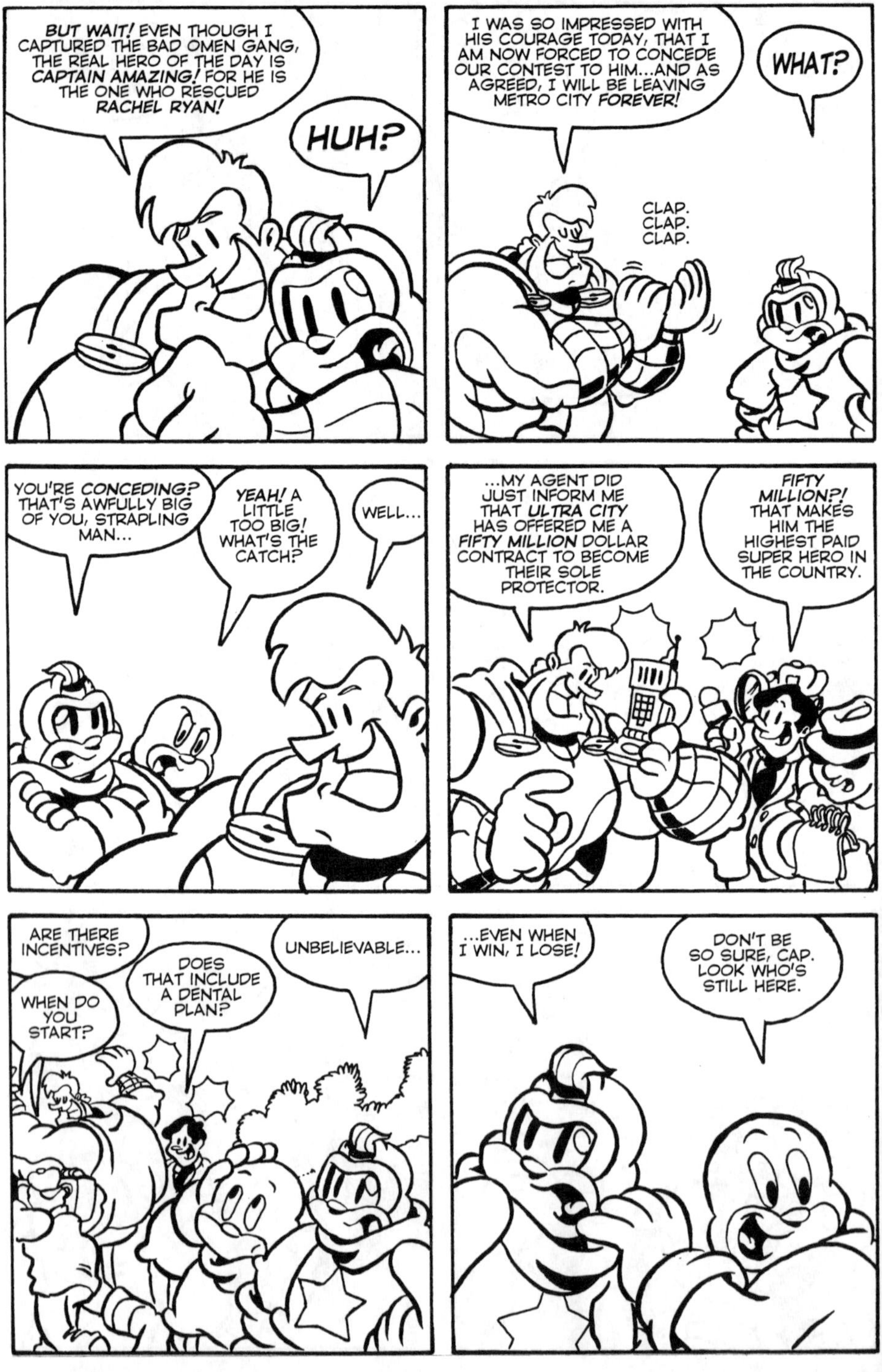

BUT WAIT! EVEN THOUGH I CAPTURED THE BAD OMEN GANG, THE REAL HERO OF THE DAY IS CAPTAIN AMAZING! FOR HE IS THE ONE WHO RESCUED RACHEL RYAN!
HUH?
I WAS SO IMPRESSED WITH HIS COURAGE TODAY, THAT I AM NOW FORCED TO CONCEDE OUR CONTEST TO HIM...AND AS AGREED, I WILL BE LEAVING METRO CITY FOREVER!
WHAT?
CLAP. CLAP. CLAP.
YOU'RE CONCEDING? THAT'S AWFULLY BIG OF YOU, STRAPLING MAN...
YEAH! A LITTLE TOO BIG! WHAT'S THE CATCH?
WELL...
...MY AGENT DID JUST INFORM ME THAT ULTRA CITY HAS OFFERED ME A FIFTY MILLION DOLLAR CONTRACT TO BECOME THEIR SOLE PROTECTOR.
FIFTY MILLION?! THAT MAKES HIM THE HIGHEST PAID SUPER HERO IN THE COUNTRY.
ARE THERE INCENTIVES?
WHEN DO YOU START?
DOES THAT INCLUDE A DENTAL PLAN?
UNBELIEVABLE...
...
...EVEN WHEN I WIN, I LOSE!
DON'T BE SO SURE, CAP. LOOK WHO'S STILL HERE.

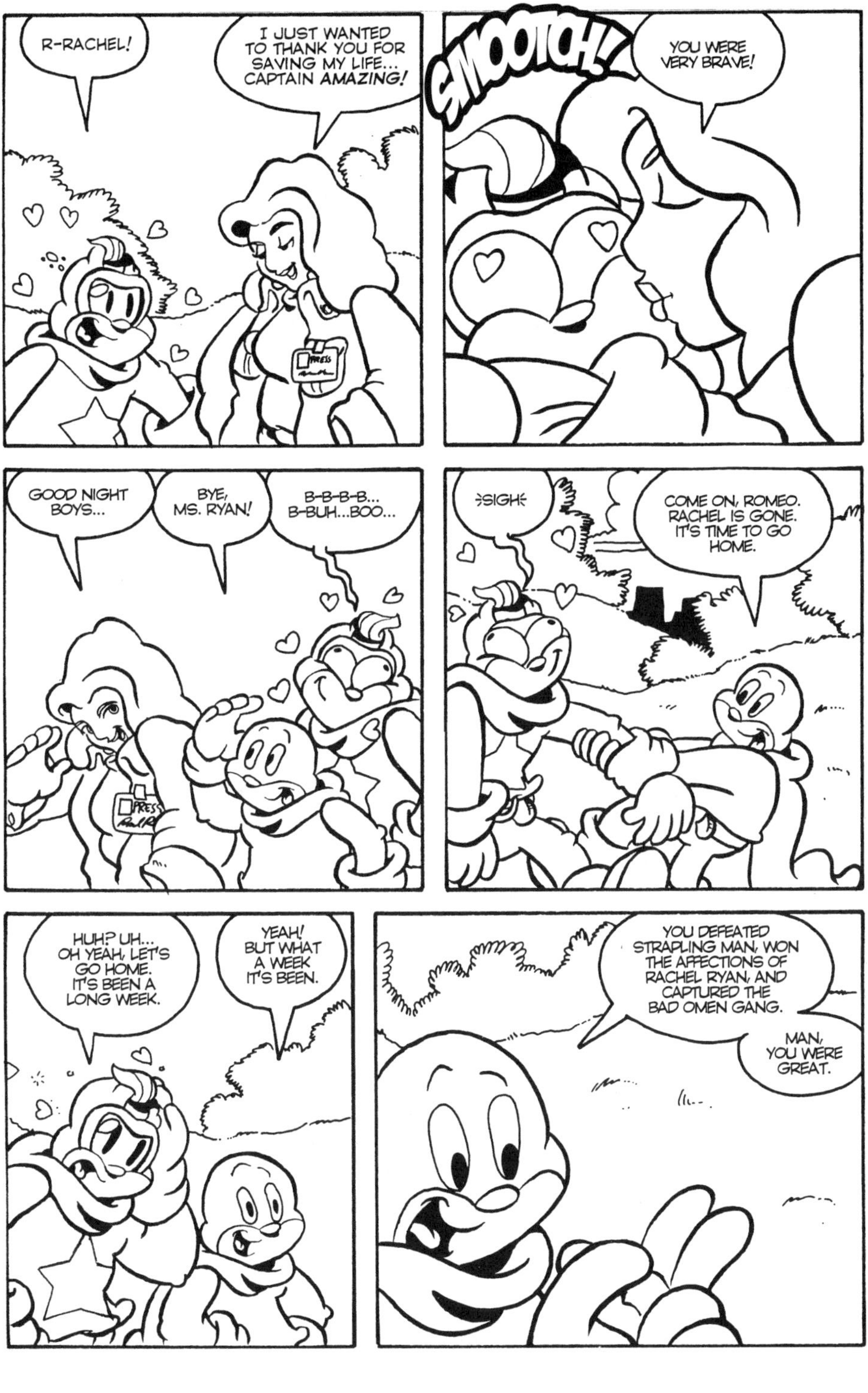
R-RACHEL!
I JUST WANTED TO THANK YOU FOR SAVING MY LIFE... CAPTAIN AMAZING!
PRESS
SMOOTCH!
YOU WERE VERY BRAVE!
GOOD NIGHT BOYS...
BYE, MS. RYAN!
B-B-B-B... B-BUH...BOO...
PRESS
SIGH
COME ON, ROMEO. RACHEL IS GONE. IT'S TIME TO GO HOME.
HUH? UH... OH YEAH, LET'S GO HOME. IT'S BEEN A LONG WEEK.
YEAH! BUT WHAT A WEEK IT'S BEEN.
YOU DEFEATED STRAPLING MAN, WON THE AFFECTIONS OF RACHEL RYAN, AND CAPTURED THE BAD OMEN GANG.
MAN, YOU WERE GREAT.

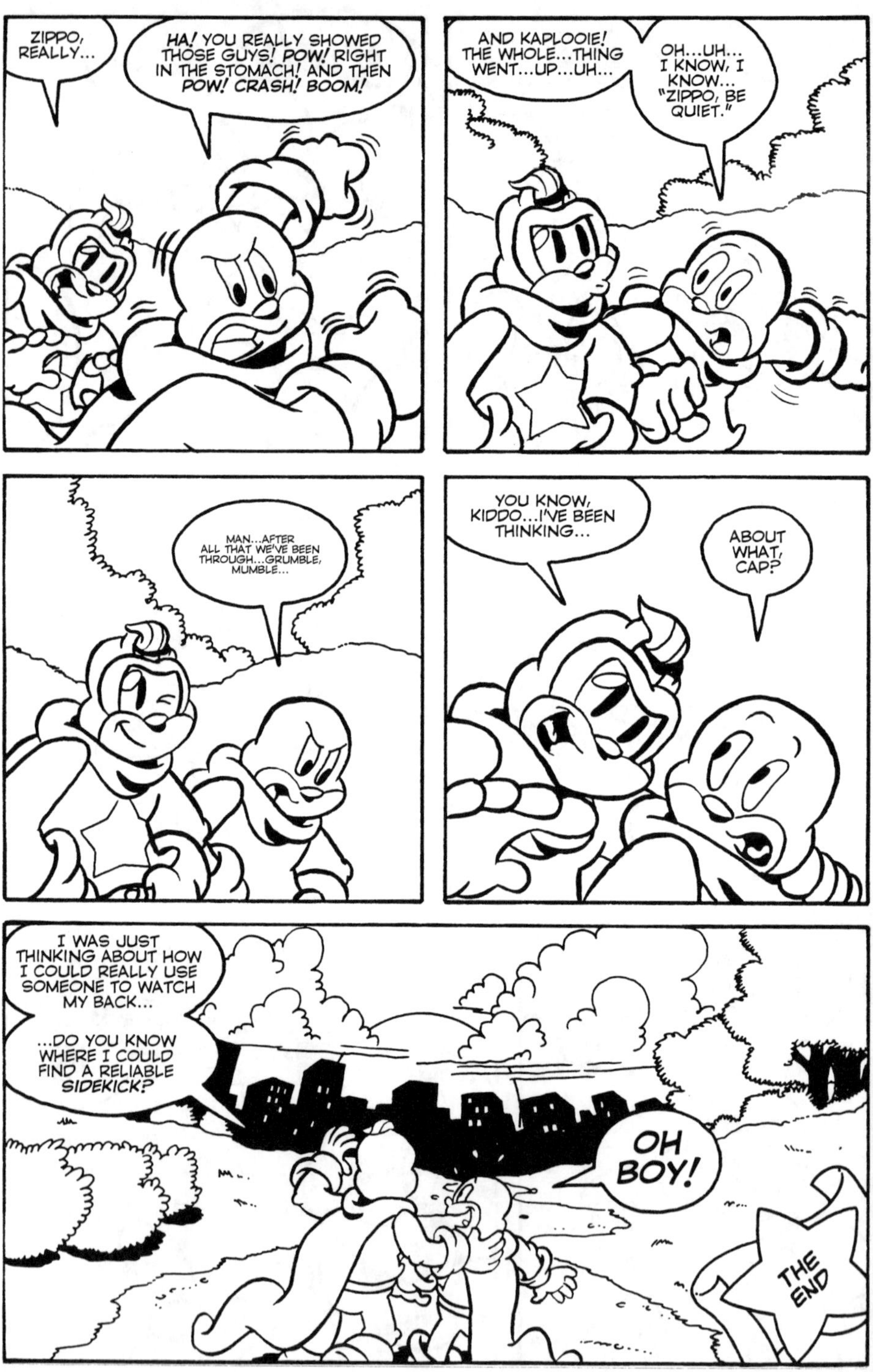

ZIPPO, REALLY...
HA! YOU REALLY SHOWED THOSE GUYS! POW! RIGHT IN THE STOMACH! AND THEN POW! CRASH! BOOM!
AND KAPLOOIE! THE WHOLE...THING WENT...UP...UH...
OH...UH... I KNOW, I KNOW... "ZIPPO, BE QUIET."
MAN...AFTER ALL THAT WE'VE BEEN THROUGH...GRUMBLE, MUMBLE...
YOU KNOW, KIDDO...I'VE BEEN THINKING...
ABOUT WHAT, CAP?
I WAS JUST THINKING ABOUT HOW I COULD REALLY USE SOMEONE TO WATCH MY BACK...
...DO YOU KNOW WHERE I COULD FIND A RELIABLE SIDEKICK?
OH BOY!
THE END

· THE COLLEGE STRIPS ·

For fun I thought I would fill the rest of the book up with some of my favorite Captain Amazing strips from my high-school and college days.

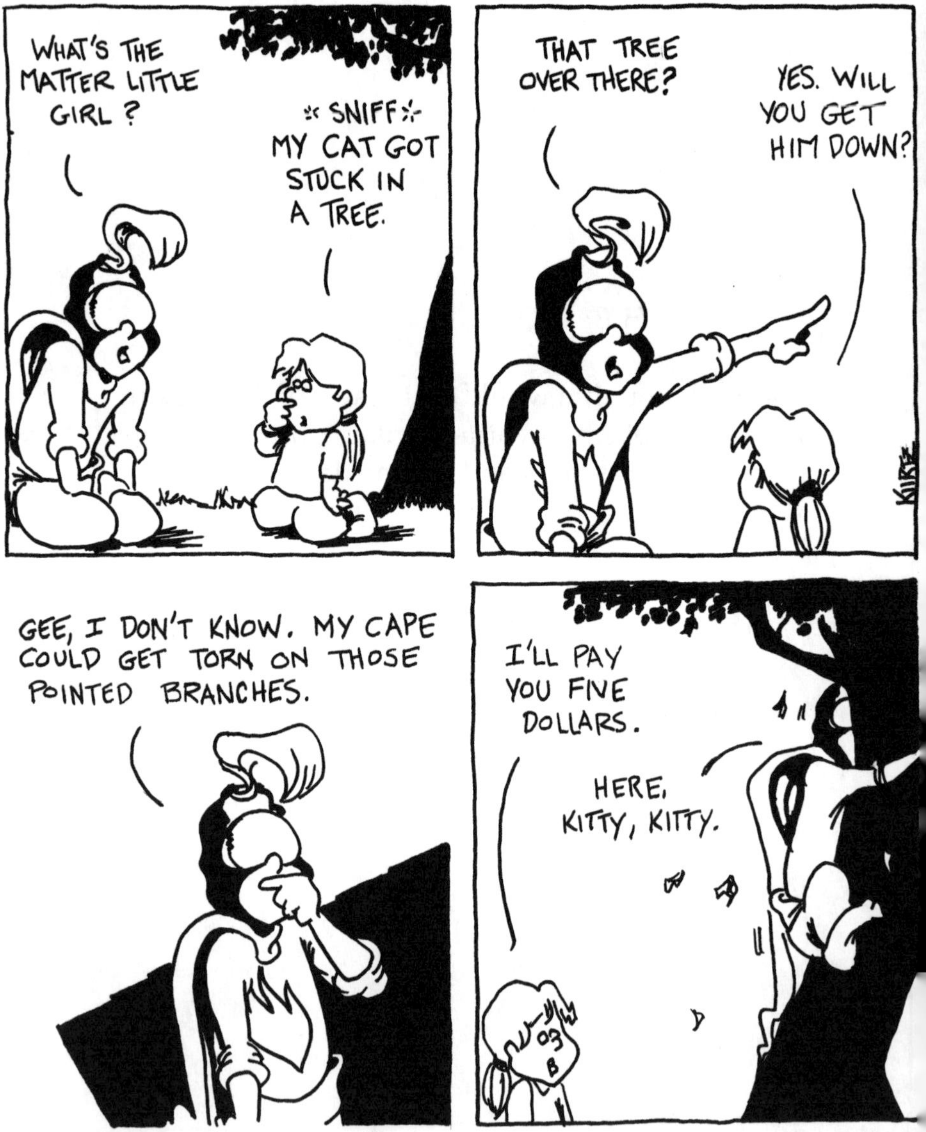
WHAT'S THE MATTER LITTLE GIRL ?
SNIFF MY CAT GOT STUCK IN A TREE.
THAT TREE OVER THERE?
YES. WILL YOU GET HIM DOWN?
GEE, I DON'T KNOW. MY CAPE COULD GET TORN ON THOSE POINTED BRANCHES.
I'LL PAY YOU FIVE DOLLARS.
HERE, KITTY, KITTY.

I created Captain Amazing in high-school (back in 1987) Back then he was known as *Captain Napalm: the sadistic super-hero.* Notice his symbol is a large flame instead of a star. Later on, I would discover that Captain Napalm was a name used in the Calvin and Hobbes comics. So when I started making comics for the college paper, I changed the character a bit and he went from being Captain Napalm to Captain Amazing.

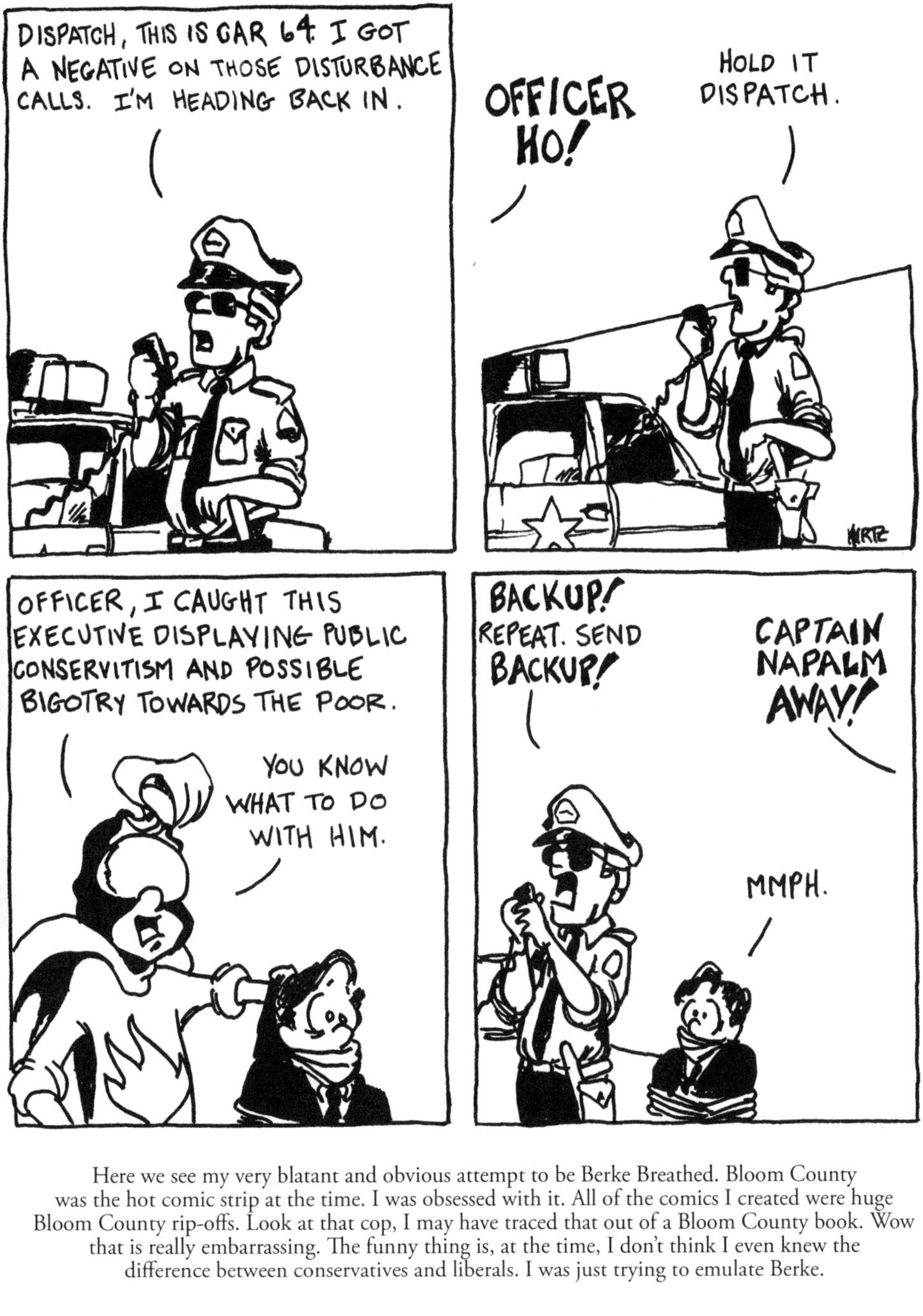
DISPATCH, THIS IS CAR 64. I GOT A NEGATIVE ON THOSE DISTURBANCE CALLS. I'M HEADING BACK IN.
OFFICER HO!
HOLD IT DISPATCH.
OFFICER, I CAUGHT THIS EXECUTIVE DISPLAYING PUBLIC CONSERVITISM AND POSSIBLE BIGOTRY TOWARDS THE POOR.
YOU KNOW WHAT TO DO WITH HIM.
BACKUP! REPEAT. SEND BACKUP!
CAPTAIN NAPALM AWAY!
MMPH.

Here we see my very blatant and obvious attempt to be Berke Breathed. Bloom County was the hot comic strip at the time. I was obsessed with it. All of the comics I created were huge Bloom County rip-offs. Look at that cop, I may have traced that out of a Bloom County book. Wow that is really embarrassing. The funny thing is, at the time, I don't think I even knew the difference between conservatives and liberals. I was just trying to emulate Berke.

LOOK MR. NAPALM. IT'S A NOBLE CAUSE REALLY, BUT...
I'M SORRY BUT YOU CAN'T GO AROUND HARASSING PEOPLE JUST BECAUSE THEY DO STUPID THINGS.
I'M SORRY OFFICER. I JUST GET ANGRY AT STUPID PEOPLE. IT WONT HAPPEN AGAIN.
PROMISE?
HEY. SCOUT'S HONOR.
I AM STUPID

Way to stick it to the man, Captain. Way to stick it to the man.
Blech!

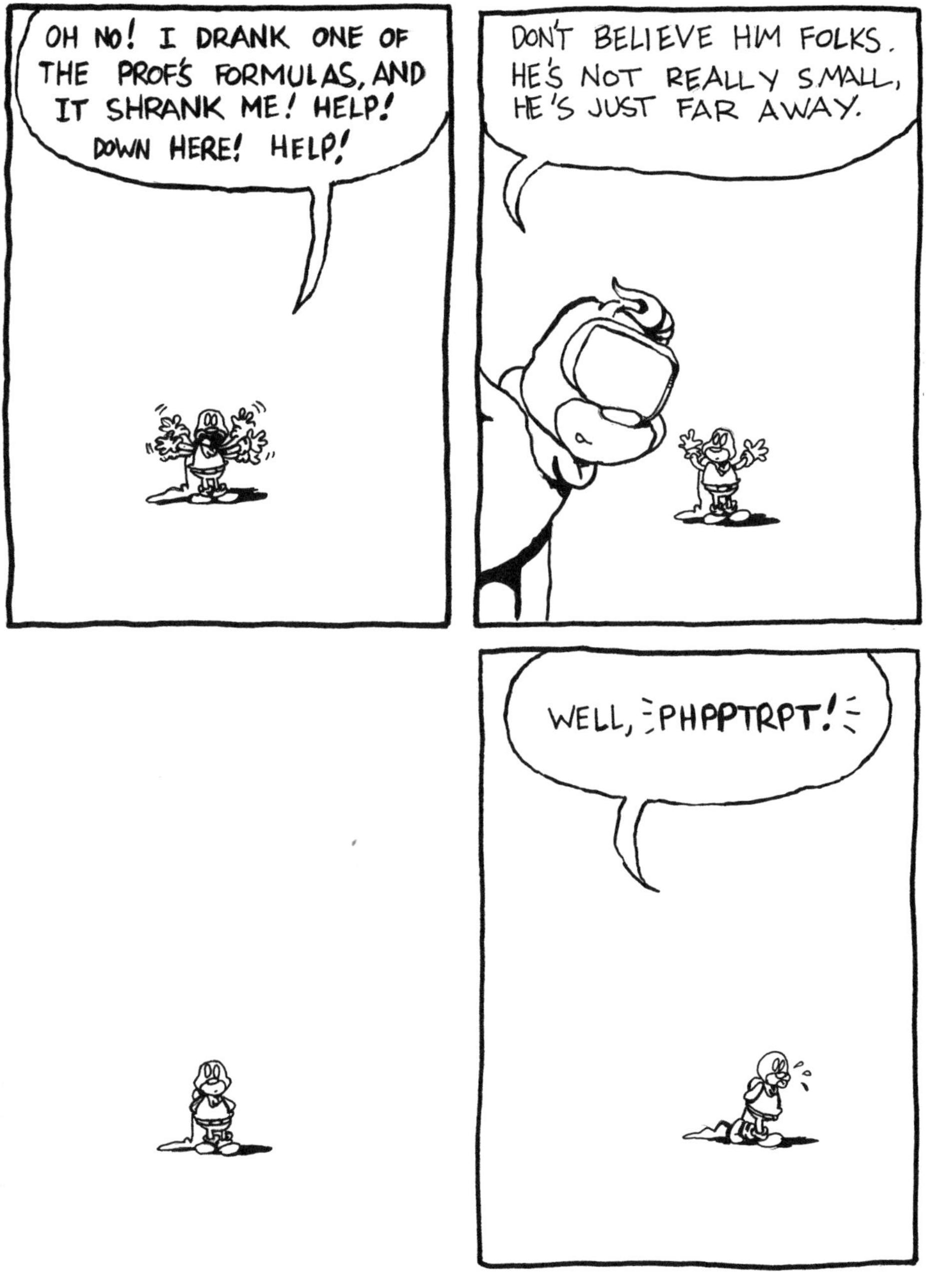
OH NO! I DRANK ONE OF THE PROF'S FORMULAS, AND IT SHRANK ME! HELP! DOWN HERE! HELP!
DON'T BELIEVE HIM FOLKS. HE'S NOT REALLY SMALL, HE'S JUST FAR AWAY.
WELL, PHPPTRPT!

Once I got to college, and began doing strips for the paper, I started to find my own unique voice. It was around this time that I met Chris Jackson who was also doing a comic strip for the same college paper.

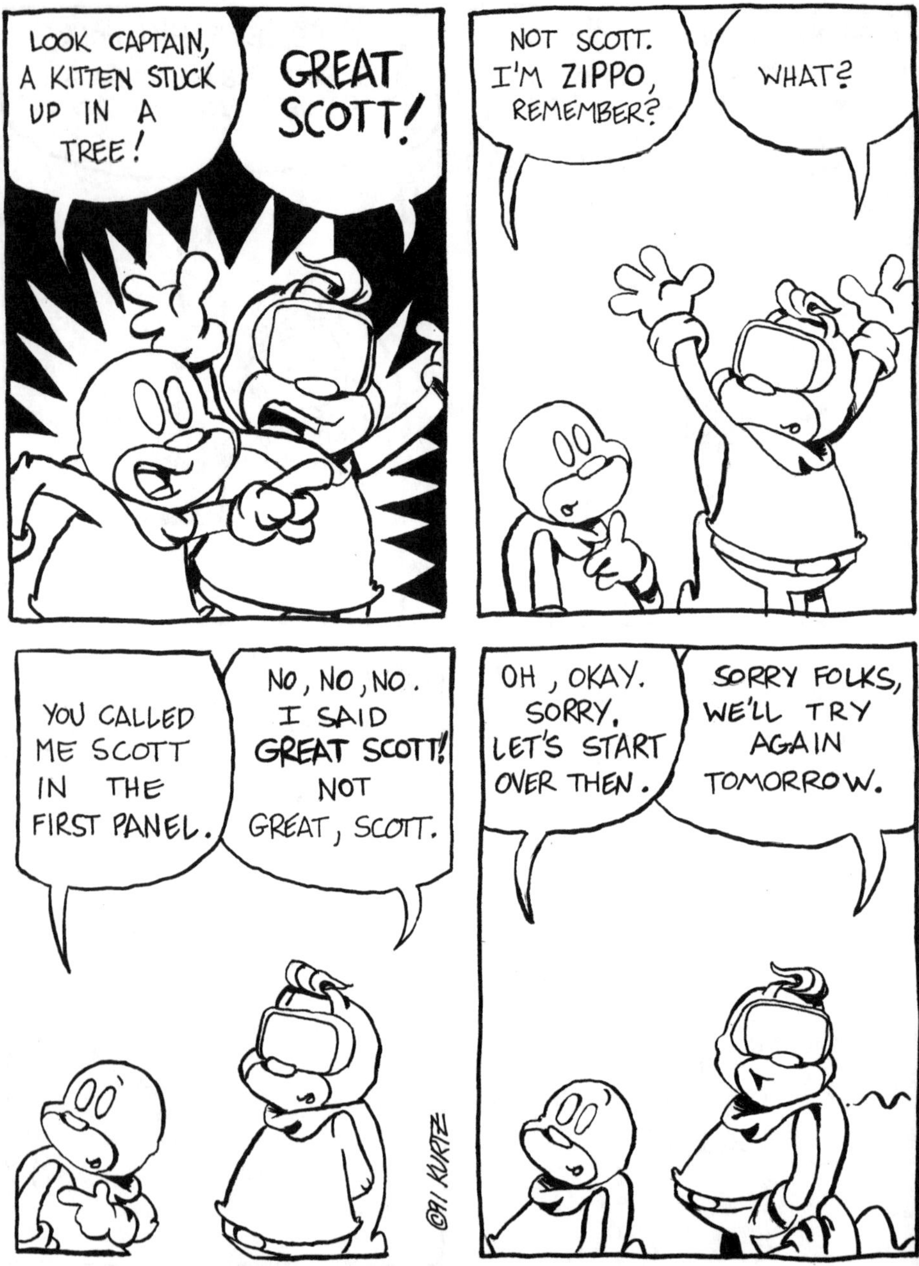
LOOK CAPTAIN, A KITTEN STUCK UP IN A TREE!
GREAT SCOTT!
NOT SCOTT. I'M ZIPPO, REMEMBER?
WHAT?
YOU CALLED ME SCOTT IN THE FIRST PANEL.
NO, NO, NO. I SAID GREAT SCOTT! NOT GREAT, SCOTT.
©91 KURTZ
OH, OKAY. SORRY. LET'S START OVER THEN.
SORRY FOLKS, WE'LL TRY AGAIN TOMORROW.

I always loved this joke.

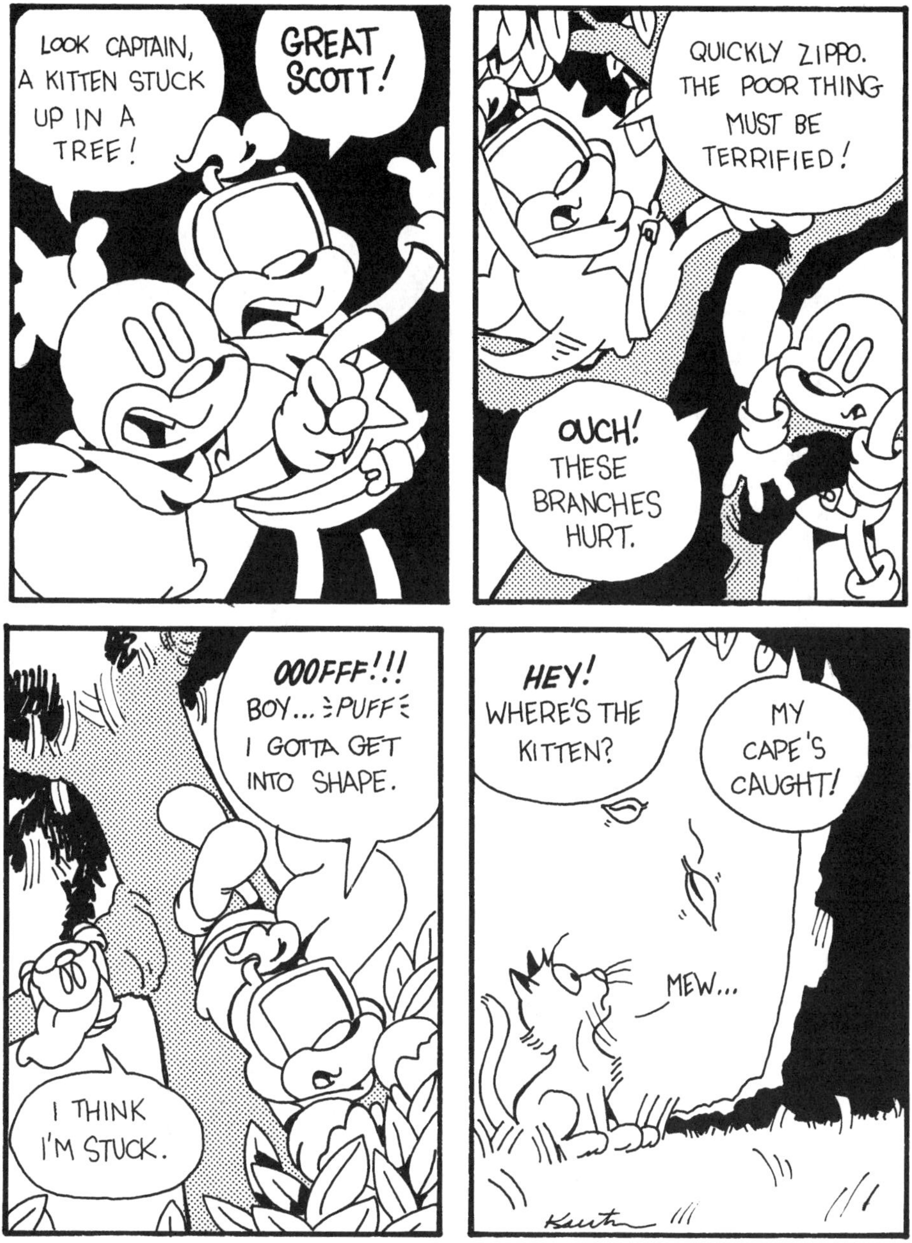
LOOK CAPTAIN, A KITTEN STUCK UP IN A TREE!
GREAT SCOTT!
QUICKLY ZIPPO. THE POOR THING MUST BE TERRIFIED!
OUCH! THESE BRANCHES HURT.
OOOFFF!!! BOY... PUFF I GOTTA GET INTO SHAPE.
I THINK I'M STUCK.
HEY! WHERE'S THE KITTEN?
MY CAPE'S CAUGHT!
MEW...

Back before photoshop and fancy computers, we used a product called ZIP-A-TONE to shade gray areas. ZIP-A-TONE was a sheer of clear sticker-paper that had a pattern of dots on it. You would cut it out, put it on your art and then use an X-acto knife to cut away what you didn't want shaded in gray. It's easier on the computer.

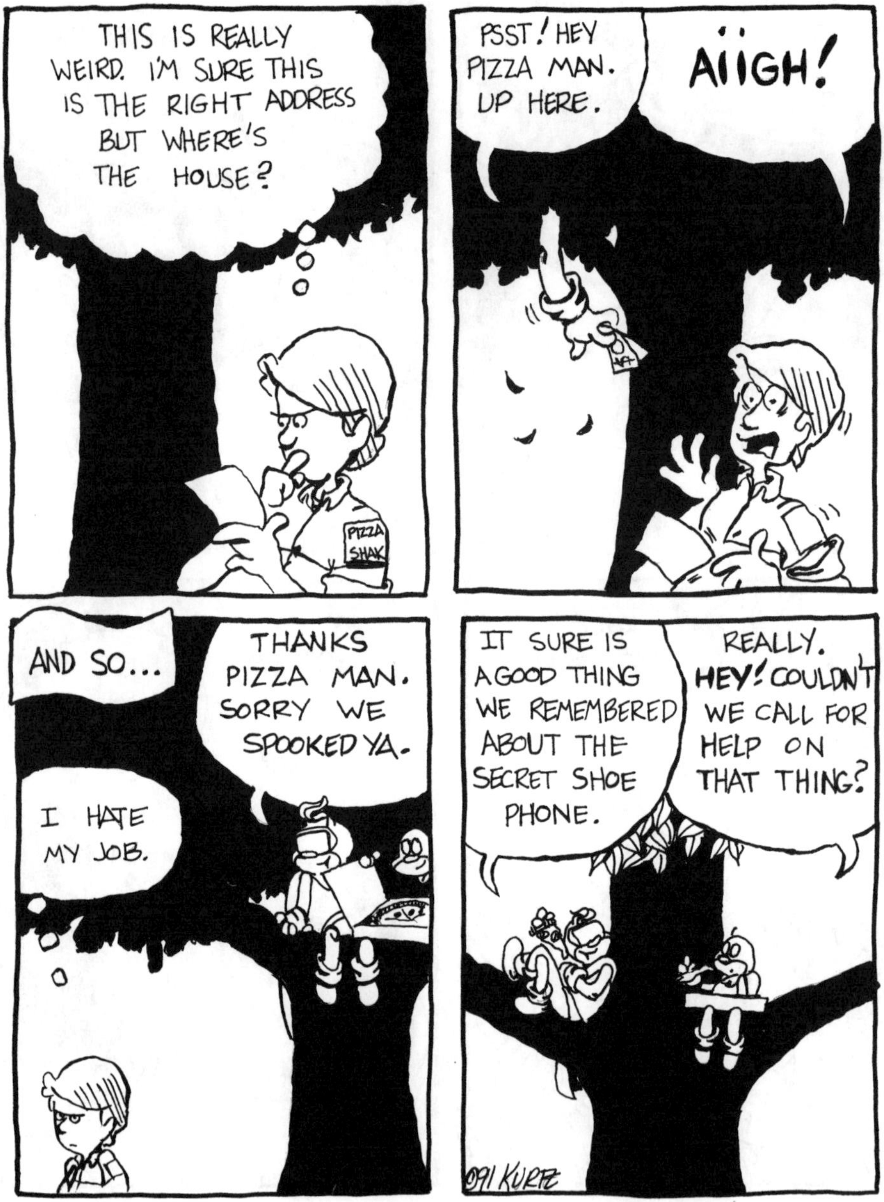
THIS IS REALLY WEIRD. I'M SURE THIS IS THE RIGHT ADDRESS BUT WHERE'S THE HOUSE?
PIZZA SHAK
PSST! HEY PIZZA MAN. UP HERE.
AIIGH!
AND SO...
THANKS PIZZA MAN. SORRY WE SPOOKED YA.
I HATE MY JOB.
IT SURE IS A GOOD THING WE REMEMBERED ABOUT THE SECRET SHOE PHONE.
REALLY. HEY! COULDN'T WE CALL FOR HELP ON THAT THING?
©91 KURTZ

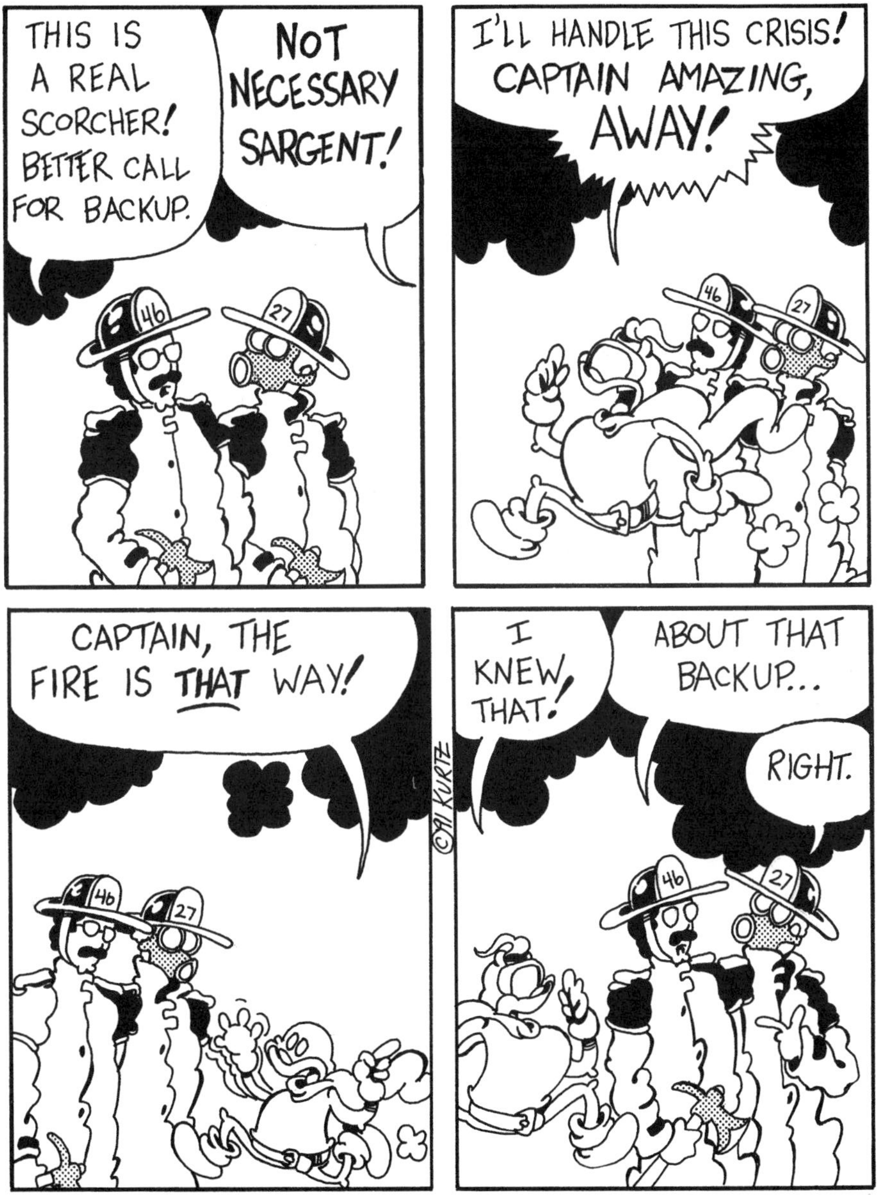
THIS IS A REAL SCORCHER! BETTER CALL FOR BACKUP.
NOT NECESSARY SARGENT!
I'LL HANDLE THIS CRISIS! CAPTAIN AMAZING, AWAY!
CAPTAIN, THE FIRE IS THAT WAY!
©91 KURTZ
I KNEW THAT!
ABOUT THAT BACKUP...
RIGHT.

This is one of many times that my father has made a guest appearance in my comic strip. Here he's the firefighter with the mustache. Love ya, Papa.

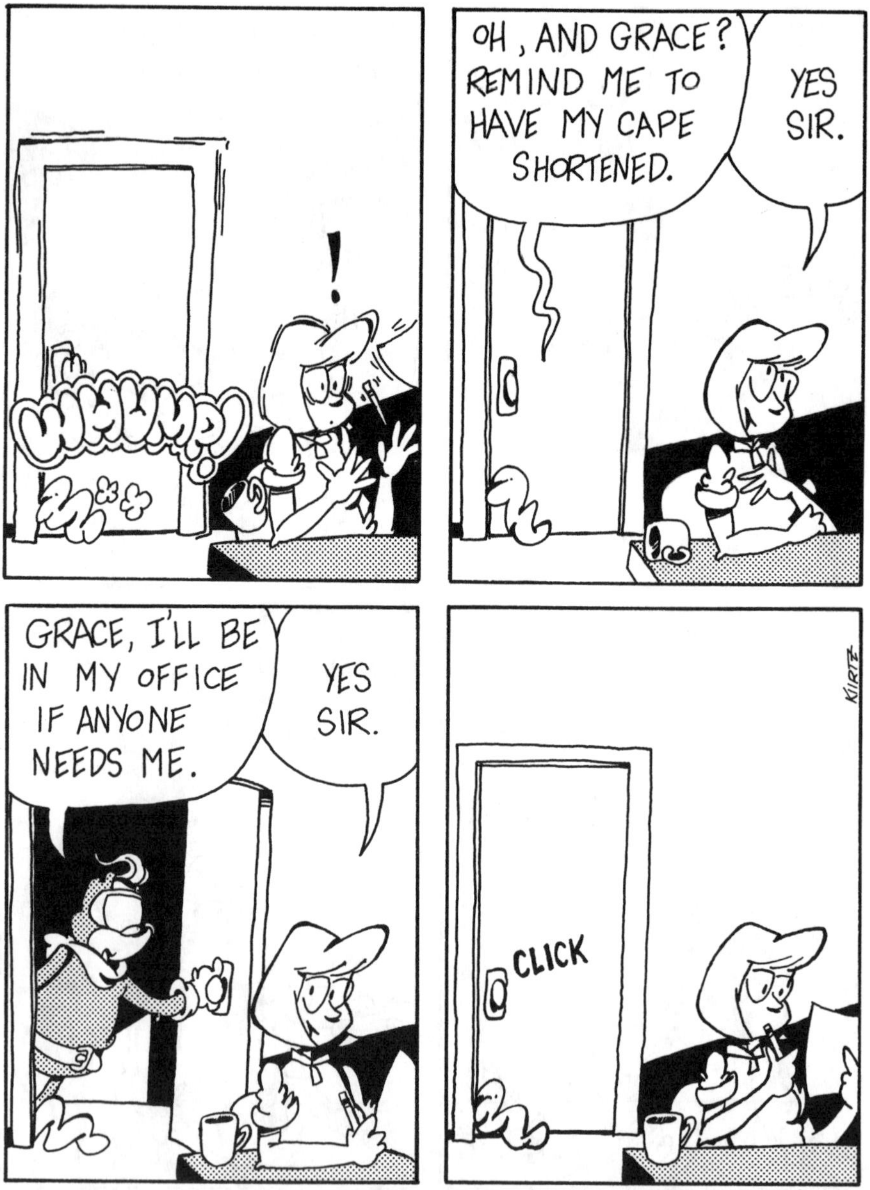
WHUMP!
!
OH, AND GRACE? REMIND ME TO HAVE MY CAPE SHORTENED.
YES SIR.
GRACE, I'LL BE IN MY OFFICE IF ANYONE NEEDS ME.
YES SIR.
KIRTZ
CLICK

Behold: the cape gag that I would go on to use over and over again. Everytime I reinvented the strip or updated the way I drew the characters I would go back and re-draw this strip.

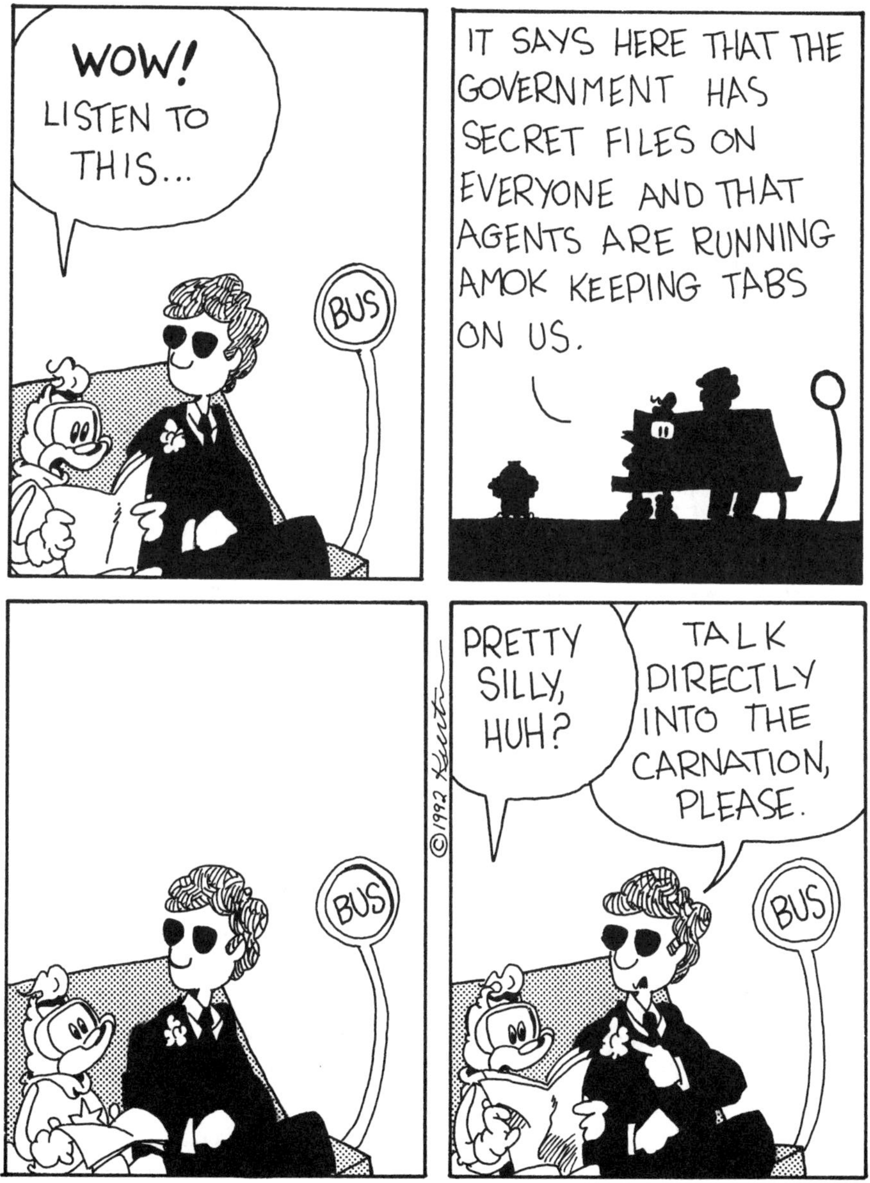
WOW! LISTEN TO THIS...
BUS
IT SAYS HERE THAT THE GOVERNMENT HAS SECRET FILES ON EVERYONE AND THAT AGENTS ARE RUNNING AMOK KEEPING TABS ON US.
BUS
©1992 Kurtz
PRETTY SILLY, HUH?
TALK DIRECTLY INTO THE CARNATION, PLEASE.
BUS

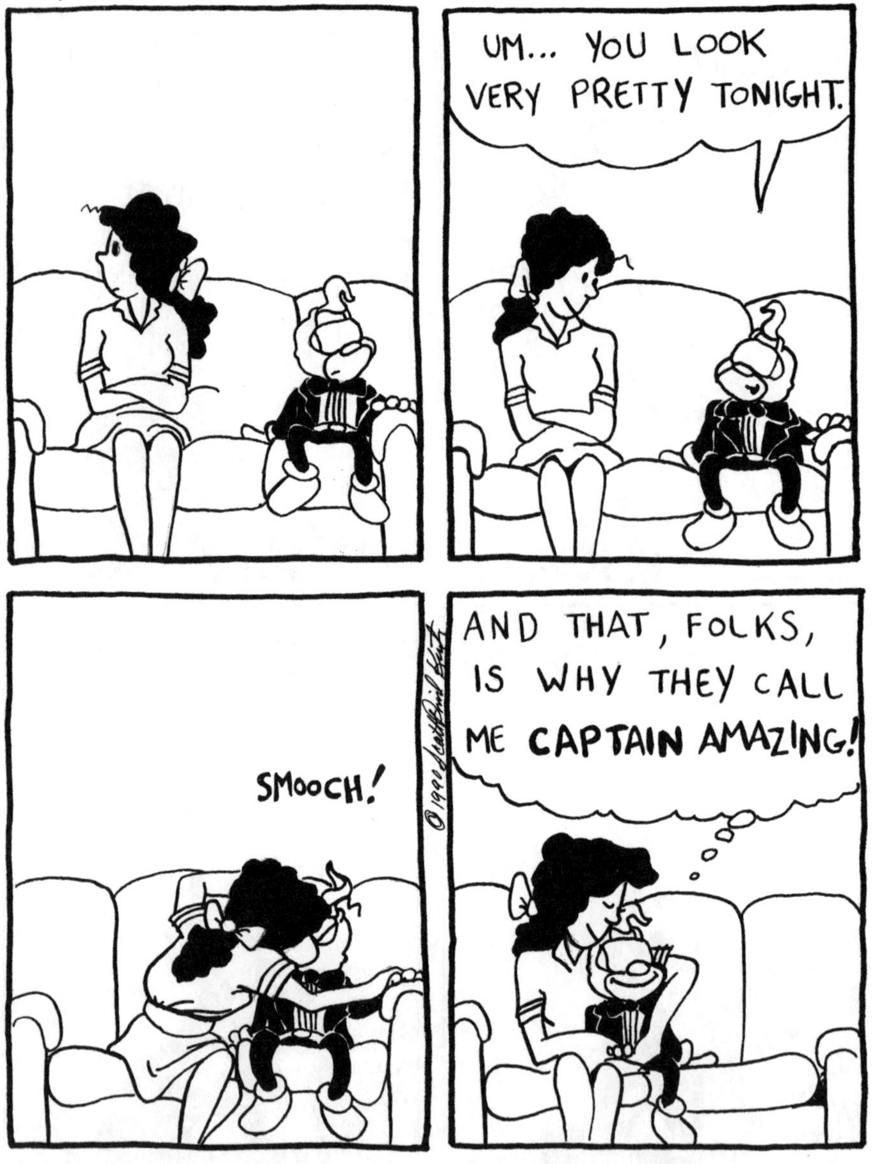
UM... YOU LOOK VERY PRETTY TONIGHT.
SMOOCH!
AND THAT, FOLKS, IS WHY THEY CALL ME CAPTAIN AMAZING!

Within the first year of being at the University of North Texas, I fell really hard for a girl. I'm not just talking about normal infatuation. I'm talking about obsessive, stalker type love. I was a nutbag over her. So of course, in the strip, the Captain got his own woman to obsess over. Her name was Elizabeth.

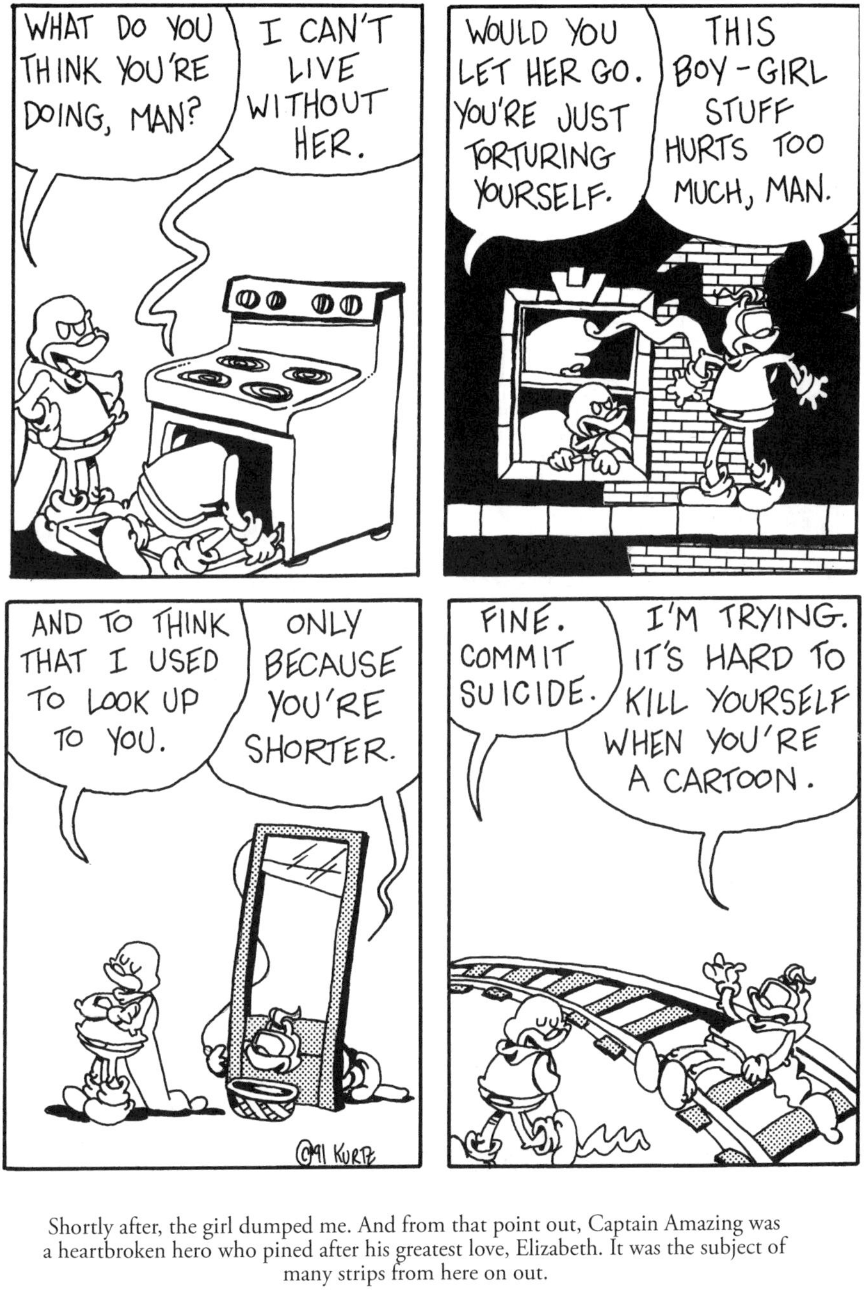
WHAT DO YOU THINK YOU'RE DOING, MAN?
I CAN'T LIVE WITHOUT HER.
WOULD YOU LET HER GO. YOU'RE JUST TORTURING YOURSELF.
THIS BOY-GIRL STUFF HURTS TOO MUCH, MAN.
AND TO THINK THAT I USED TO LOOK UP TO YOU.
ONLY BECAUSE YOU'RE SHORTER.
©91 KURTZ
FINE. COMMIT SUICIDE.
I'M TRYING. IT'S HARD TO KILL YOURSELF WHEN YOU'RE A CARTOON.

Shortly after, the girl dumped me. And from that point out, Captain Amazing was a heartbroken hero who pined after his greatest love, Elizabeth. It was the subject of many strips from here on out.

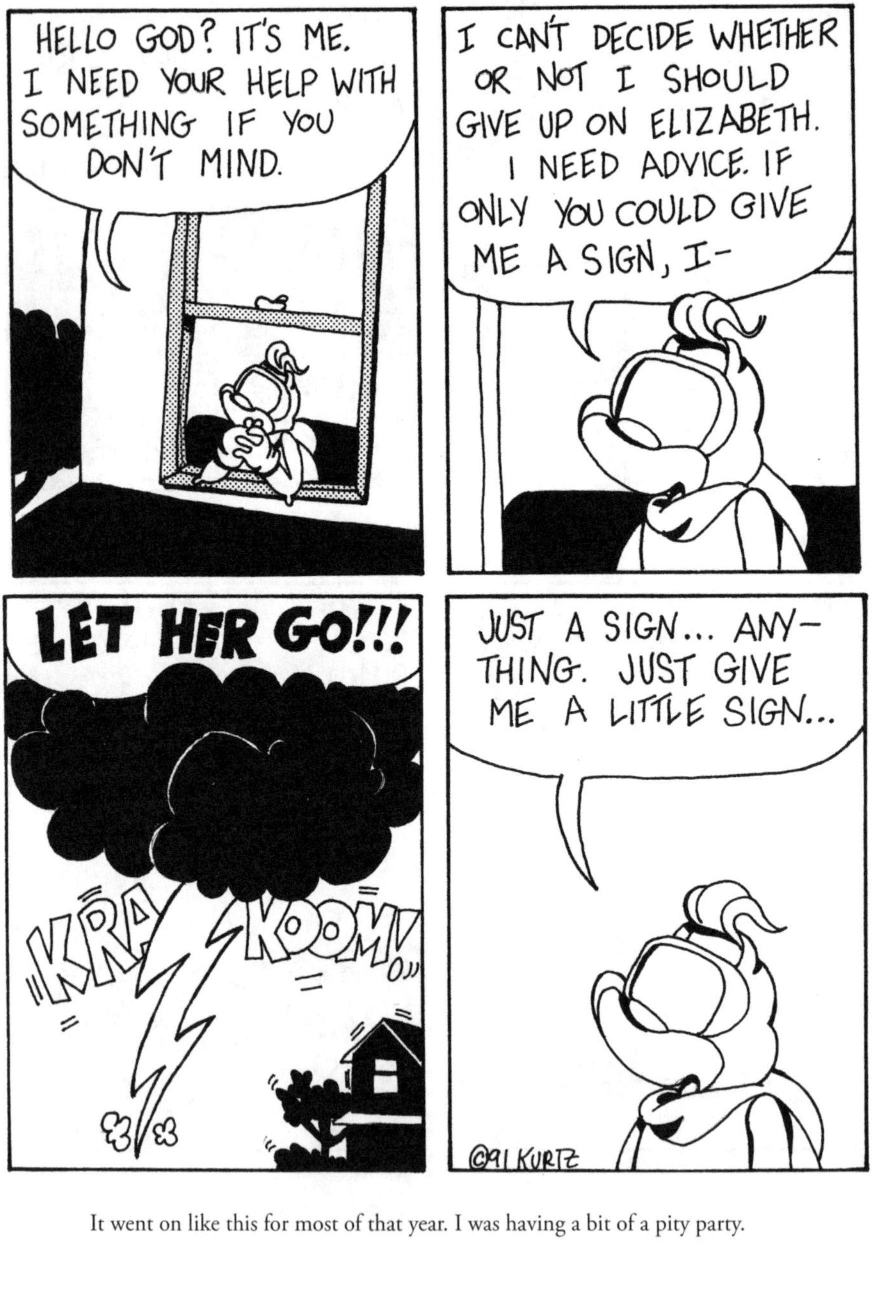
HELLO GOD? IT'S ME. I NEED YOUR HELP WITH SOMETHING IF YOU DON'T MIND.
I CAN'T DECIDE WHETHER OR NOT I SHOULD GIVE UP ON ELIZABETH. I NEED ADVICE. IF ONLY YOU COULD GIVE ME A SIGN, I-
LET HER GO!!!
KRA KOOM!
JUST A SIGN... ANY-THING. JUST GIVE ME A LITTLE SIGN...
©91 KURTZ

It went on like this for most of that year. I was having a bit of a pity party.

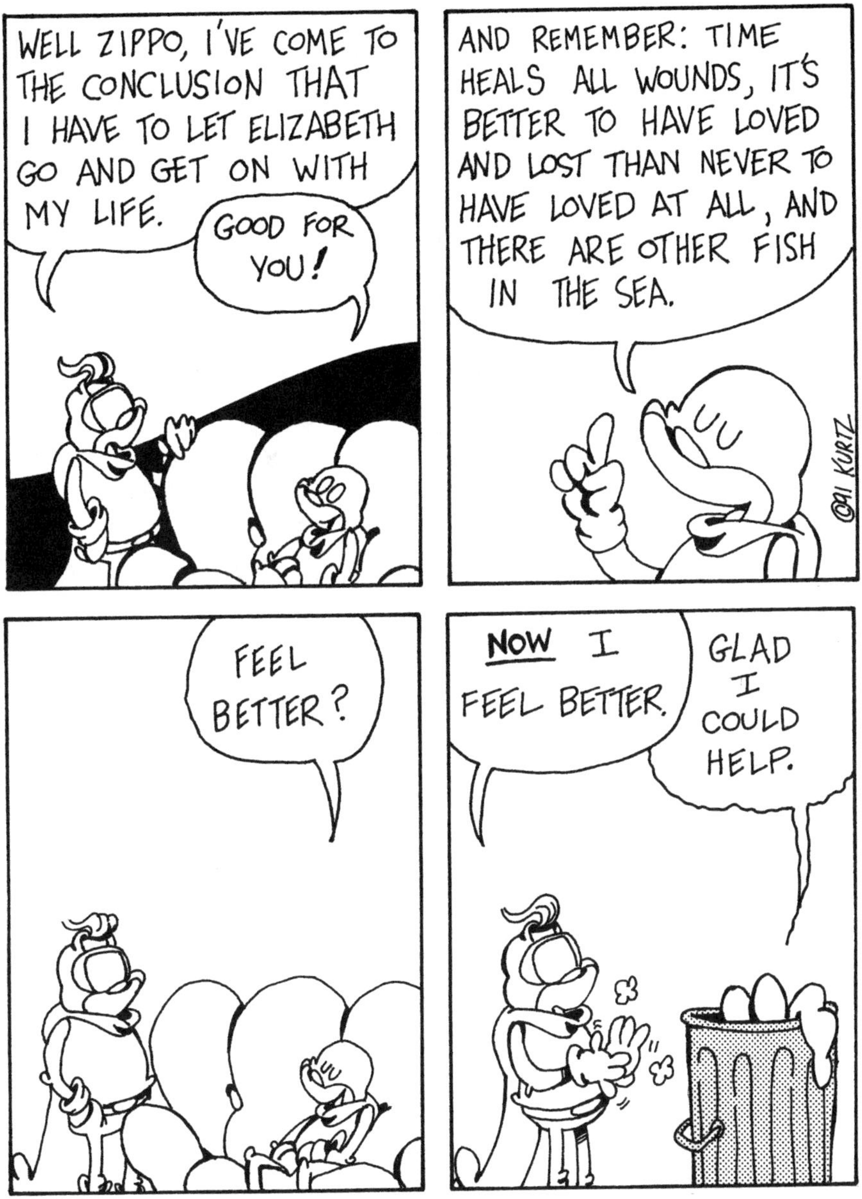
WELL ZIPPO, I'VE COME TO THE CONCLUSION THAT I HAVE TO LET ELIZABETH GO AND GET ON WITH MY LIFE.
GOOD FOR YOU!
AND REMEMBER: TIME HEALS ALL WOUNDS, IT'S BETTER TO HAVE LOVED AND LOST THAN NEVER TO HAVE LOVED AT ALL, AND THERE ARE OTHER FISH IN THE SEA.
©91 KURTZ
FEEL BETTER?
NOW I FEEL BETTER.
GLAD I COULD HELP.

...and on and on....

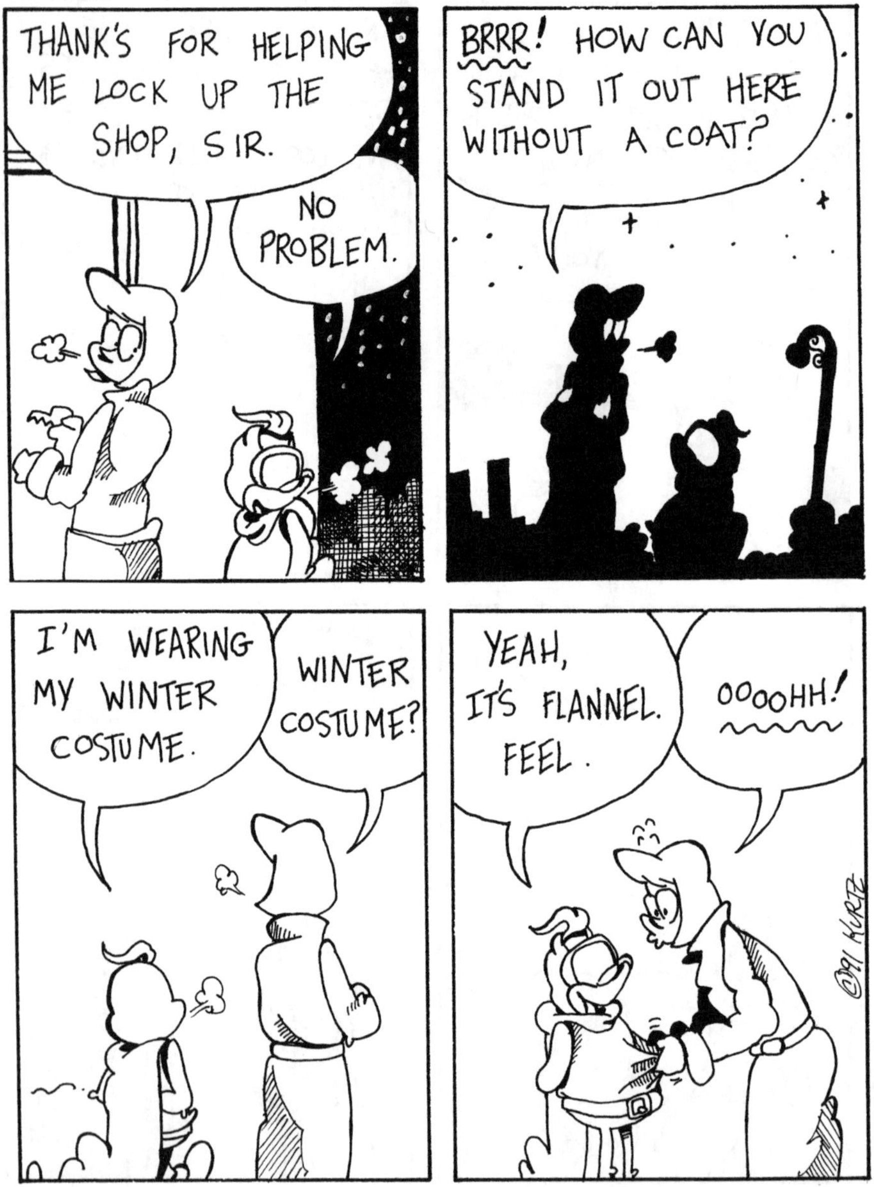
THANK'S FOR HELPING ME LOCK UP THE SHOP, SIR.
NO PROBLEM.
BRRR! HOW CAN YOU STAND IT OUT HERE WITHOUT A COAT?
I'M WEARING MY WINTER COSTUME.
WINTER COSTUME?
YEAH, IT'S FLANNEL. FEEL.
OOOOHH!
©91 KURTZ

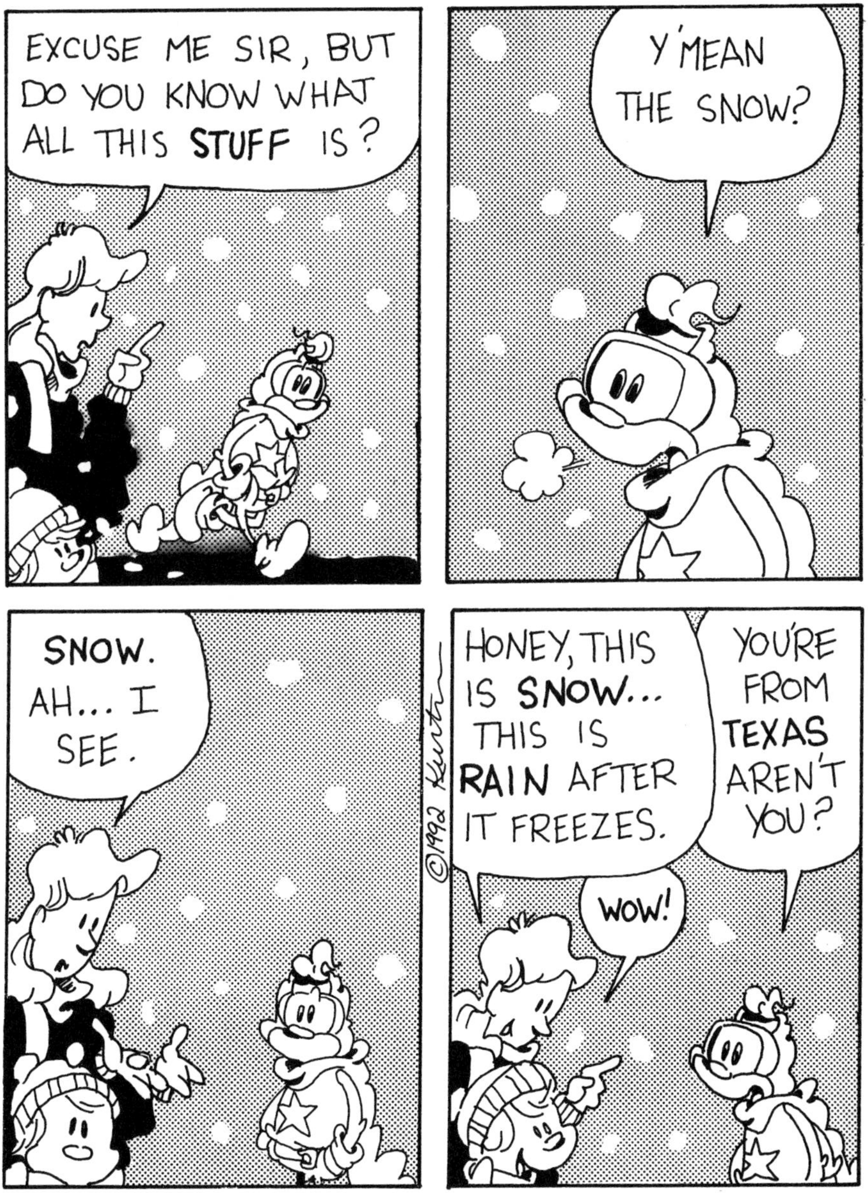
EXCUSE ME SIR, BUT DO YOU KNOW WHAT ALL THIS STUFF IS?
Y'MEAN THE SNOW?
SNOW. AH... I SEE.
©1992 Kurtz
HONEY, THIS IS SNOW... THIS IS RAIN AFTER IT FREEZES.
YOU'RE FROM TEXAS AREN'T YOU?
WOW!

Eventually, Chris suggested that I give the Captain eyeballs. Can you believe I was reluctant to try this? It didn't take long for me to realize that Chris was right.

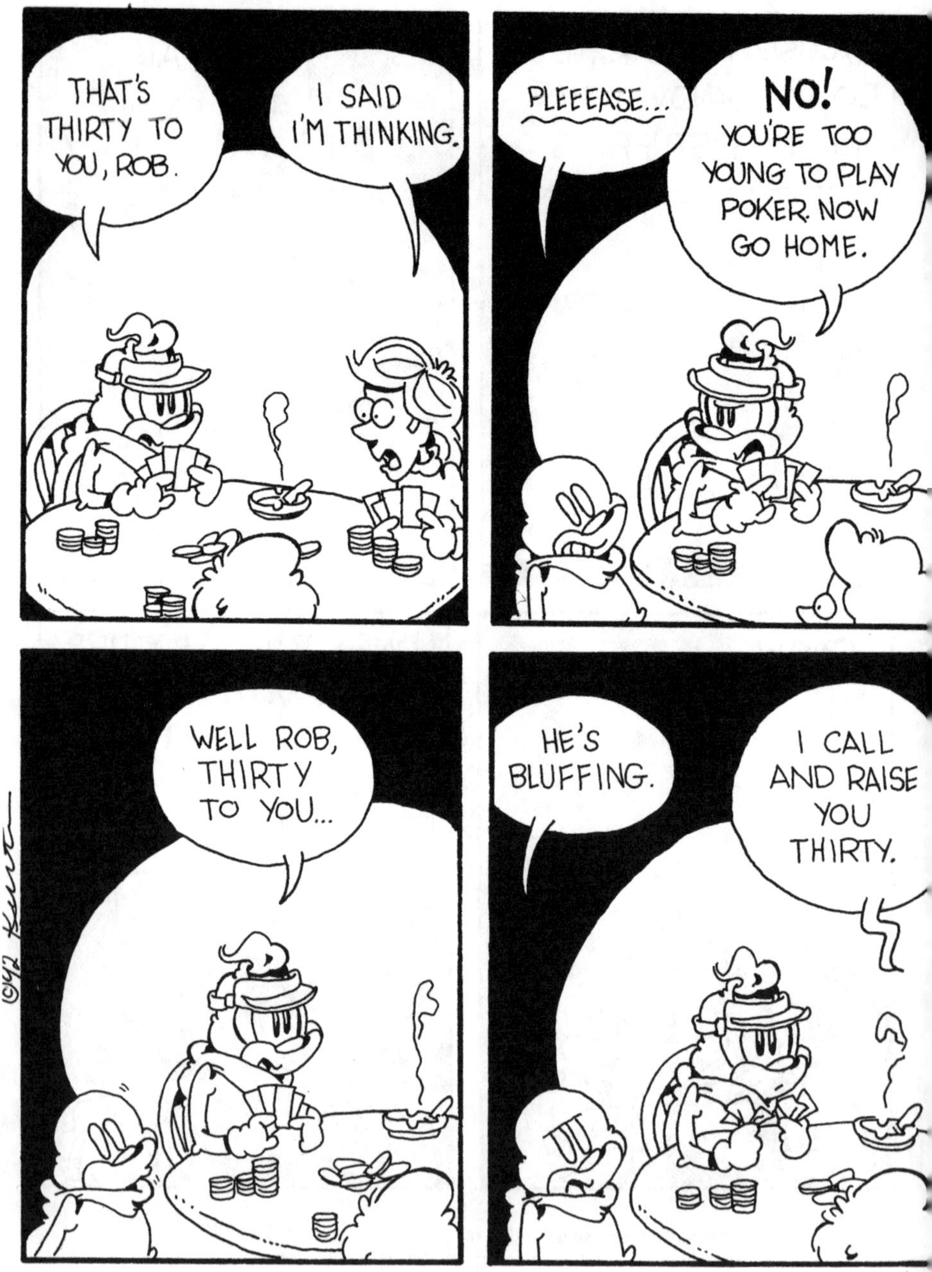
THAT'S THIRTY TO YOU, ROB.
I SAID I'M THINKING.
PLEEEEASE...
NO! YOU'RE TOO YOUNG TO PLAY POKER. NOW GO HOME.
WELL ROB, THIRTY TO YOU...
HE'S BLUFFING.
I CALL AND RAISE YOU THIRTY.
©'92 Kent

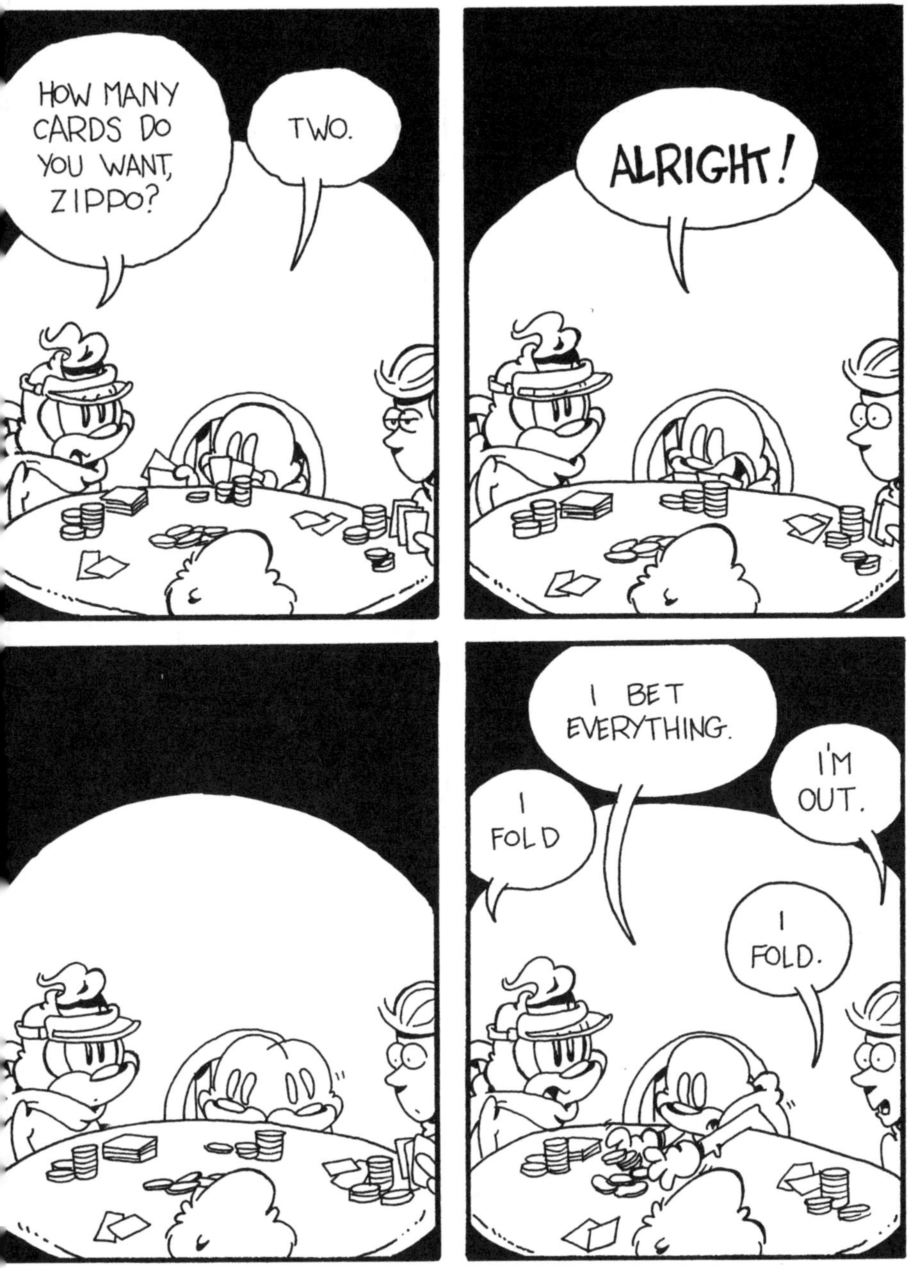
HOW MANY CARDS DO YOU WANT, ZIPPO?
TWO.
ALRIGHT!
I BET EVERYTHING.
I FOLD
I'M OUT.
I FOLD.

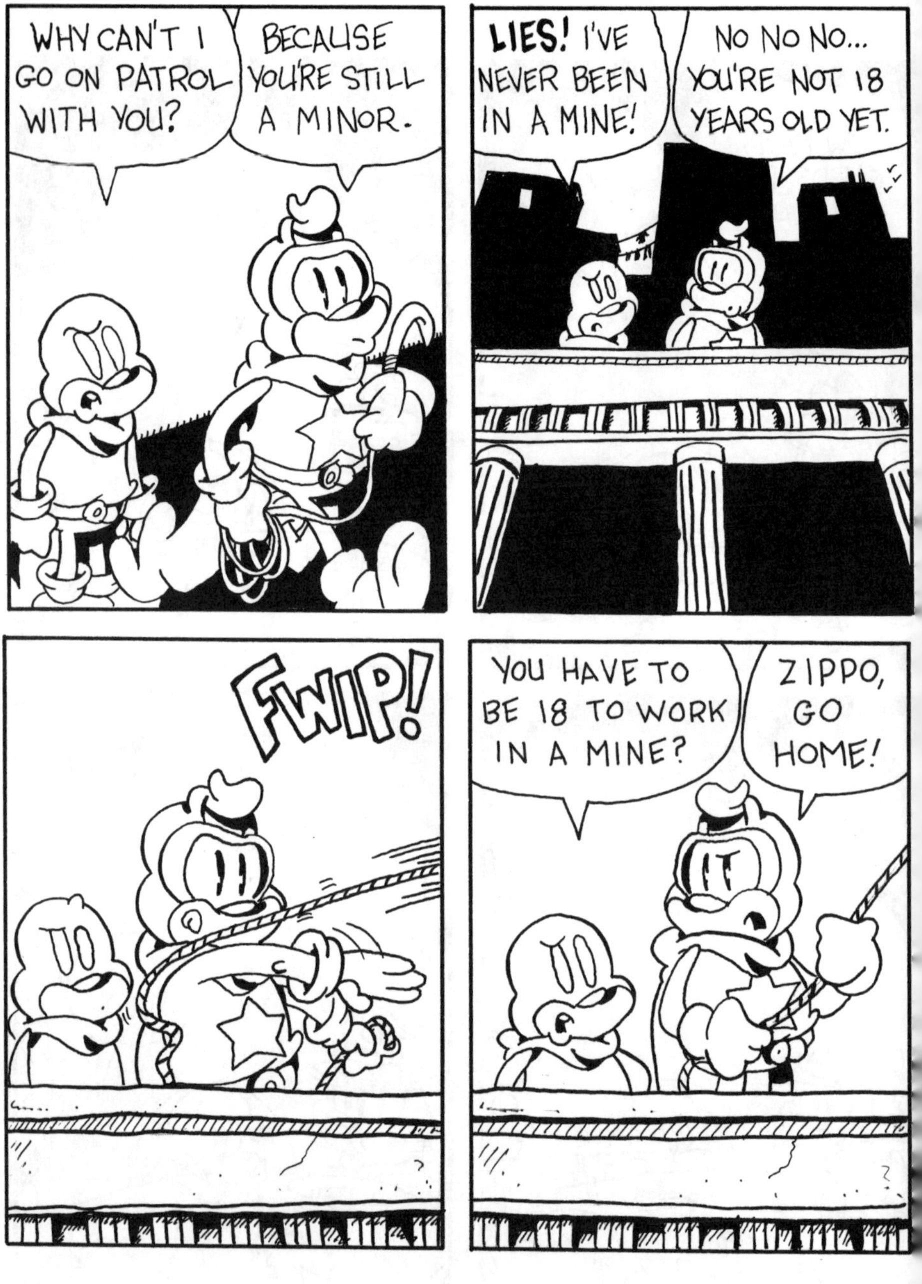
WHY CAN'T I GO ON PATROL WITH YOU?
BECAUSE YOU'RE STILL A MINOR.
LIES! I'VE NEVER BEEN IN A MINE!
NO NO NO... YOU'RE NOT 18 YEARS OLD YET.
FWIP!
YOU HAVE TO BE 18 TO WORK IN A MINE?
ZIPPO, GO HOME!

After College, I sent out one submission package to the syndicates for Captain Amazing. They all rejected the strip but I did get one personal letter of encouragement. It was just enough to keep my delusion alive.

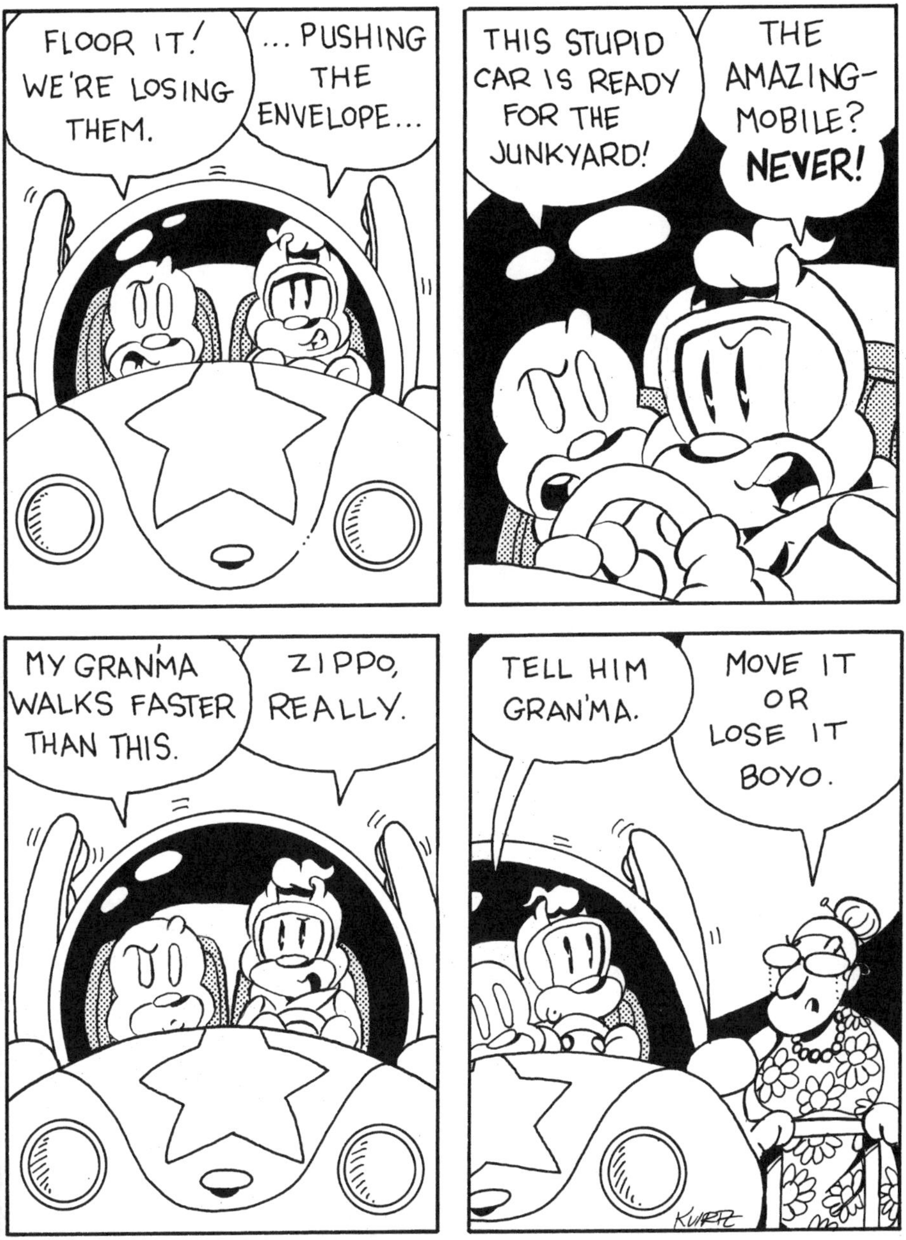
FLOOR IT! WE'RE LOSING THEM.
... PUSHING THE ENVELOPE...
THIS STUPID CAR IS READY FOR THE JUNKYARD!
THE AMAZING-MOBILE? NEVER!
MY GRAN'MA WALKS FASTER THAN THIS.
ZIPPO, REALLY.
TELL HIM GRAN'MA.
MOVE IT OR LOSE IT BOYO.
KURTZ

Luckily, Image Comics has much lower standards than the national syndicates. Thank you all so much for buying this book!
-Scott

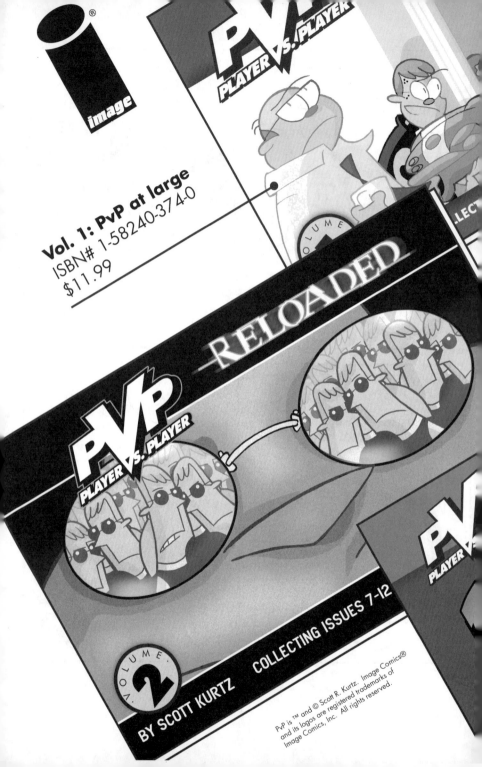

Vol. 1: PvP at large
ISBN# 1-58240-374-0
$11.99

RELOADED

VOLUME 2

BY SCOTT KURTZ

COLLECTING ISSUES 7-12

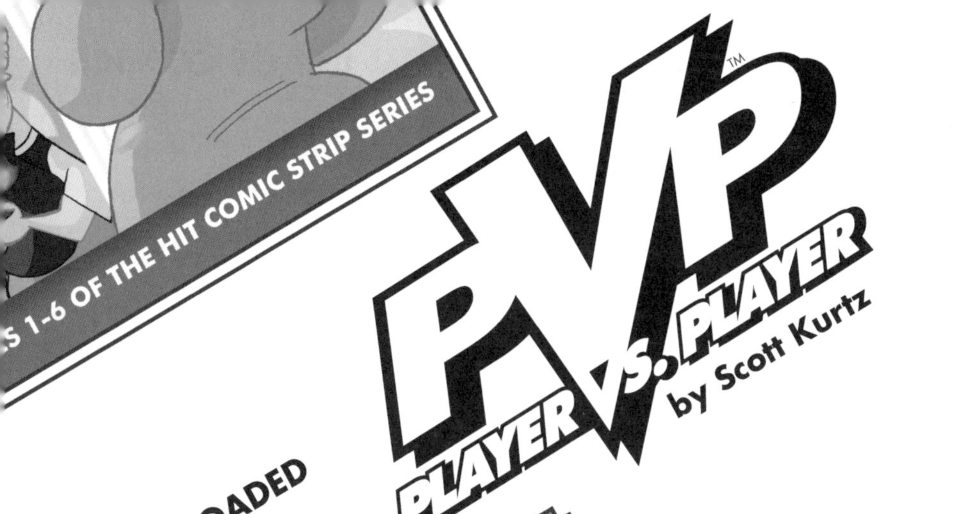

S 1-6 OF THE HIT COMIC STRIP SERIES

PvP™ PLAYER VS. PLAYER

by Scott Kurtz

Vol. 2: PvP RELOADED
ISBN# 1-58240-433-X
$11.95

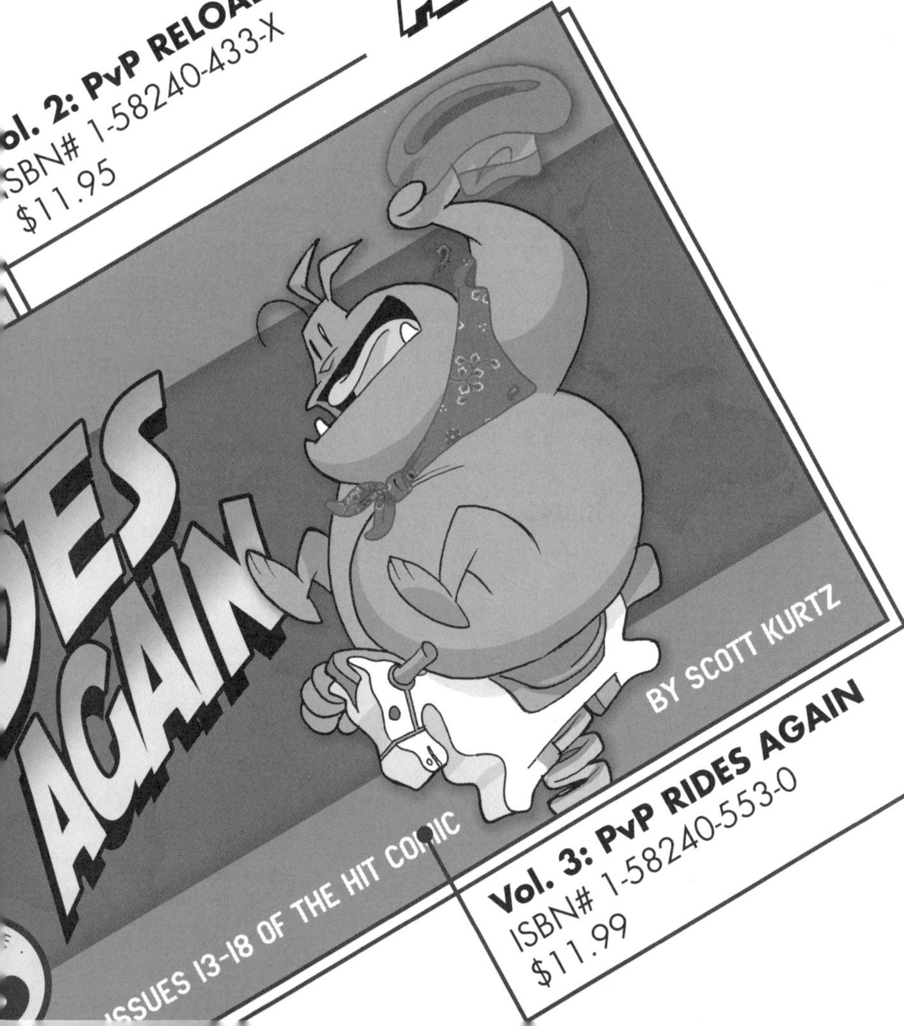

DES AGAIN
BY SCOTT KURTZ
ISSUES 13-18 OF THE HIT COMIC

Vol. 3: PvP RIDES AGAIN
ISBN# 1-58240-553-0
$11.99

MORE GREAT BOOKS FROM IMAGE COMICS

For a comic shop near you carrying graphic novels from Image Comics, please call toll free:
1-888-COMIC-BOOK

A DISTANT SOIL
VOL. 1: THE GATHERING TP
ISBN# 1887279512
$19.95
VOL. 2: THE ASCENDANT TP
ISBN# 1582400180
$28.95
VOL.3: ARIA TP
ISBN# 1582403619
$16.95
VOL. 4: CODA TP
ISBN# 158240478x
$17.99

AGE OF BRONZE
VOL. 1: A THOUSAND SHIPS TP
ISBN# 1582402000
$19.95
VOL. 2: SACRIFICE HC
ISBN# 1582403600
$29.95

THE AMAZING JOY BUZZARDS, VOL. 1 TP
ISBN# 1582404984
$11.95

BAD IDEAS COLLECTED! TP
ISBN# 158240531x
$12.99

THE BLACK FOREST
VOL. 1 GN
ISBN# 1582403503
$9.95
VOL. 2: CASTLE OF SHADOWS GN
ISBN# 1582405611
$6.99

CREASED
ISBN# 1582404216
$9.95

DAWN
VOL. 1:
LUCIFER'S HALO NEW ED TP
ISBN# 1582405689
$17.99
VOL. 1: LUCIFERS HALO
SUPPLEMENTAL BOOK TP
ISBN# 1582405697
$12.99

DEATH, JR TP
ISBN# 1582405263
$14.99

EARTHBOY JACOBUS GN
ISBN# 1582404925
$17.95

FEAR AGENT, VOL. 1 TP: RE-IGNITION
ISBN# 1582406189
$9.99

FOUR-LETTER WORLDS
ISBN# 1582404399
$12.95

GIRLS
VOL 1: CONCEPTION TP
ISBN# 1582405298
$14.99
VOL 2: EMERGENCE TP
ISBN# 1582406081
$14.99

GRRL SCOUTS
VOL. 1 TP
ISBN# 1582403163
$12.95
VOL. 2: WORK SUCKS TP
ISBN# 1582403430
$12.95

GUN FU, VOL 1 TP
ISBN# 1582405212
$14.95

HAWAIIAN DICK, VOL. 1: BYRD OF PARADISE TP
ISBN# 1582403171
$14.95

HEAVEN, LLC GN
ISBN# 1582403511
$12.95

KANE
VOL. 1:
GREETINGS FROM NEW EDEN TP
ISBN# 1582403406
$11.95
VOL. 2: RABBIT HUNT TP
ISBN# 1582403554
$12.95
VOL. 3: HISTORIES TP
ISBN# 1582403821
$12.95
VOL. 4: THIRTY NINTH TP
ISBN# 1582404682
$16.95
VOL. 5: UNTOUCHABLE RICO
COSTAS & OTHER STORIES TP
ISBN# 1582405514
$13.99

LONG HOT SUMMER GN
ISBN# 158240559x
$7.99

MIDNIGHT NATION TP
ISBN# 158240460
$24.99

MINISTRY OF SPACE
ISBN# 1582404232
$12.99

PUT THE BOOK BACK ON THE SHELF: A BELLE & SEBASTIAN ANTHOLOGY
ISBN# 1582406006
$19.99

RIDE, VOL. 1 TP
ISBN# 1582405220
$9.99

RONIN HOOD OF THE 47 SAMURAI
ISBN# 1582405557
$9.99

SEA OF RED
VOL. 1:
NO GRAVE BUT THE SEA TP
ISBN# 1582405379
$8.95
VOL. 2: NO QUARTER
ISBN# 1582405417
$11.99

TOMMYSAURUS REX GN
ISBN# 1582403953
$11.95

ULTRA: SEVEN DAYS TP
ISBN# 1582404836
$17.99

THE WICKED WEST GN
ISBN# 1582404143
$9.95

THE WALKING DEAD
VOL. 1: DAYS GONE BYE TP
ISBN# 1582403589
$12.95
VOL. 2: MILES BEHIND US TP
ISBN# 1582404135
$12.95
VOL. 3:
SAFETY BEHIND BARS TP
ISBN# 1582404879
$12.95
VOL. 4:
THE HEART'S DESIRE TP
ISBN# 1582405301
$12.99